T0163721

LETTING GOOD THINGS RUN WILD

Praise for
LETTING GOOD THINGS RUN WILD

The principles in *Letting Good Things Run Wild* are not only deeply edifying on a personal level, but they are incredibly fruitful for business. As a church planter, author, and small business owner there is not a single area of my life that has not been improved by these truths. Every reader will agree that this book is clear, thought-provoking, and practical. Whether you're a business owner overseeing day-to-day operations, a minister in the local church, or a CEO of a multi-million dollar corporation, you will benefit from this book.

—**Amy Gannett,** author of *Fix Your Eyes: How Theology Shapes Our Worship* and founder of Tiny Theologians

Dr. Greg is a man of great faith, action, and solid results. Over the years I have been privileged to see him build two successful businesses and help other leaders in his community grow along the way. In *Letting Good Things Run Wild*, he dunks myths concerning stewardship and growth and makes a compelling connection between the two. He also shares key tools with you that you can use to live out your own vision for life and work. In essence, by reading and applying the wisdom shared in this book, you too can *let good things run wild*!

—**Tim Enochs,** *New York Times* bestselling author and founder of NEWLife Leadership

"For physical training is of some value but godliness has value for all things, holding promise for both the present life and the life to come." Athletes know how important physical training and great training partners are when pursuing excellence. Business leaders understand the importance of great associates. In his book, *Letting Good Things Run Wild*, Dr. Gilbaugh brings timeless, biblical truth to practical application. Dr. Greg has been an elite athlete, playing Division 1 football; he has a doctorate degree and runs successful businesses. He coaches and consults leaders. He has been the key elder in a growing church for twenty-plus years. Most importantly, he has a wonderful family. How does he do it? He does it by soaking in the truth of God's Word and allowing it to permeate every aspect of his life. We don't need a list of priorities. Dr. Greg teaches us how to have God in the center of it all, a model to live by. I am challenged to be and do better!

—**Lincoln McIlravy**, three-time NCAA wrestling
champion, four-time gold medalist US National Freestyle,
three-time World Cup gold medalist, and Founder of
Serve 20:28, Inc. Hospitality Properties

As a leader or worker, you can make an impact on the company you work in or lead. Greg shares the template on how to do that with practical tips and on-target theology. You'll be well prepared to make a difference in the marketplace as you soak in the principles in this book.

—**Greg Leith,** CEO, Convene

For over forty years, I have known Greg as a friend, father, husband, and lover of Jesus. Now, as an author, he has put impactful words to a desperate audience of men needing to know how to make Christ known in the marketplace world.

—**Keith Chancey,** director, Kanakuk K7 Kamp
and president, Kanakuk Institute

LETTING GOOD THINGS RUN WILD

The Integration of Faith and Business Creating a Deeper Faith, a Better Business, and Greater Impact

Greg Gilbaugh

NASHVILLE

NEW YORK • LONDON • MELBOURNE • VANCOUVER

LETTING GOOD THINGS RUN WILD
The Integration of Faith and Business Creating a Deeper Faith, a Better Business, and Greater Impact

© 2022 Greg Gilbaugh

All rights reserved. No portion of this book may be reproduced, stored in a retrieval system, or transmitted in any form or by any means—electronic, mechanical, photocopy, recording, scanning, or other—except for brief quotations in critical reviews or articles, without the prior written permission of the publisher.

Published in New York, New York, by Morgan James Publishing. Morgan James is a trademark of Morgan James, LLC. www.MorganJamesPublishing.com

Proudly distributed by Ingram Publisher Services.

Unless otherwise noted, Scripture quotations taken from the (NASB®) New American Standard Bible®, Copyright © 1960, 1971, 1977, 1995, 2020 by The Lockman Foundation. Used by permission. All rights reserved. www.lockman.org.

Scripture quotations marked (NIV) are taken from the Holy Bible, New International Version®, NIV®. Copyright © 1973, 1978, 1984, 2011 by Biblica, Inc.™ Used by permission of Zondervan. All rights reserved worldwide. www.zondervan.com The "NIV" and "New International Version" are trademarks registered in the United States Patent and Trademark Office by Biblica, Inc.™

Morgan James BOGO™

A **FREE** ebook edition is available for you or a friend with the purchase of this print book.

CLEARLY SIGN YOUR NAME ABOVE

Instructions to claim your free ebook edition:
1. Visit MorganJamesBOGO.com
2. Sign your name CLEARLY in the space above
3. Complete the form and submit a photo of this entire page
4. You or your friend can download the ebook to your preferred device

ISBN 978-1-63195-759-8 paperback
ISBN 978-1-63195-760-4 ebook
Library of Congress Control Number:
2021917561

Cover Design by:
Rachel Lopez
www.r2cdesign.com

Morgan James is a proud partner of Habitat for Humanity Peninsula and Greater Williamsburg. Partners in building since 2006.

Get involved today! Visit MorganJamesPublishing.com/giving-back

To the Lord Jesus—
For leading me through a real fire, floods, and disability
to bring me to a place that I didn't think was possible.
Allow me to steward well and finish strong.

and to my wife Laura—
who constantly reminded me through it all
that it's that "covenant, one flesh thing."

TABLE OF CONTENTS

Acknowledgments   xi

Introduction   xiii

Section One: **Gaining a Deeper Faith That**   **1**
                  Will Impact Your Business

Chapter One   The Theology of Work: Starting Off   3
                  on the Right Foundation

Chapter Two   Calling   16

Chapter Three   Stewardship   26

Chapter Four   Character and Integrity in   38
                  the Marketplace

Chapter Five   Skill and Service   49

Section Two: **Building a Better Business**   **61**

Chapter Six   Making a Life Plan with a Priority of One   63

Chapter Seven   Business Vision and What Could Be   79

Chapter Eight   Your Business Mission: Stewardship   96

Chapter Nine   Business Tools to Get the Job Done   111

Section Three: **Greater Impact**   **129**

Chapter Ten   Leadership As a Way of Life   131

Chapter Eleven   The Seasons of Leadership   140

Chapter Twelve   The Conclusion   162

About the Author   167

ACKNOWLEDGMENTS

Being a science major whose only experience in writing is creating a yearly Christmas letter, I never thought that writing a book was a possibility. Yet here I am with my passion now on paper, hopefully, to bring some encouragement to others and help them on their journeys.

I have received so much help along the way with this project. To my bride Laura, you have been a consistent source of encouragement and reassurance, not only in the creation of this book but also in transitioning into this next season of our lives. It's been quite a ride thus far, and I look forward to finishing strong with you. Princess, you mean everything to me.

Amy Gannett, you are an accomplished author, writer, theology junkie, blogger, speaker, wife of a great man, and a mama. I am proud to call you daughter and am honored to be your father. You are so much like your mama in that you brought me so much encouragement during this project that I was able to get into the end zone. My bucket list still includes a time when you and I can speak at a conference together.

Tim Enochs, I hired you as an executive coach five years ago to help me navigate through a ten-year plan. Along the way, you have become a close friend and brother. Early on, you told me that you thought I had what it takes to become a coach. You also said that I "had a book inside me that needed to come out." At first, I thought that you were just being nice. Little did I realize that you were impacting my life. You encouraged me to coach others, and I did. You encouraged me to write and then connected me with Morgan James Publishing. You took a personal interest in making sure this project became a reality. Thanks, Coach. You get a helmet sticker for this.

David Hancock and the team at Morgan James, you took a chance on someone that had no writing experience or skills but understood the passion that I wanted to put on the pages. I am still astonished that you took a chance on me and allowed me to join your team. Thanks for your vote of confidence and for bringing this project to life.

And to the team at The Family Dental Center and The Children's Dental Center. You not only gave me time to think and write, but you show that what I get to write about is not just theory; it really works. Thank you for working so hard at being exceptional and making good things happen.

INTRODUCTION

Larry (not his real name) and I had started meeting over coffee and our conversations centered around being a person of faith in the marketplace. After working through a few topics and getting our next refill, Larry began to open up about some of his struggles. He told me how he feels that people in his community group at church just don't understand some of the real issues that he faces as a business owner. He is carrying a weight of responsibility that many others in the church do not have, and as a result, he feels a little isolated ". . . not understood . . . and to be honest, alone." He reports similar feelings in his business environment. Larry has a deep faith and allegiance to God that most in his business world do not share. He wrestles with bringing aspects of faith into his business decisions, but again, he feels isolated, misunderstood, and very much alone.

I cannot tell you how many times I have heard this story. I want to forget the number of years that I have lived this story. This is a common reality to many people of faith, who find themselves living in the world of business leadership. When someone cannot connect the most important aspect of their life (their faith) with the area of their life they spend most of xiv | LETTING GOOD THINGS RUN WILD

their waking hours in (their business), the results are enormous. Enormously bad. The outcome is the loss of potential impact and productivity. Indeed, I have seen this movie before, and it usually has the same familiar ending.

My parents moved to a nice retirement area in Florida several years ago, and I had been there to visit quite a few times. While with them, I met some of their friends, neighbors, and my dad's golfing buddies. A number of these men had impressive business backgrounds prior to their retirements: a C-suite position for a major automotive manufacturer, a regional director for a restaurant chain covering twenty states, an insurance entrepreneur who owned multiple offices and had numerous agents working for him—so much so that I truly believed if he blew his nose, the green stuff that would come out would be one-hundred-dollar bills. These men also went to church with my parents. They, too, were people who had loved Jesus for years and still confessed allegiance to Him in their "golden years." And yet, in this church of 1000 people, these men and women's spiritual acts of service were limited to handing out bulletins on Sunday morning or maybe leading a men's Bible study.

What an absolute waste.

In the season of life that can potentially be the most influential . . . the most fruitful . . . the most impactful, so many of these saints are sitting on the bench, falsely believing that the life God has given them—along with the skills, talent, and experience that He has led them through—and their value to the Kingdom have become nothing more than handing out paper and writing a monthly check to the church.

Finishing strong has been replaced by coasting along.

And guys like Larry are going to be joining them soon.

This is the common theme of those who struggle to connect their faith with their business interests. Lots of potential that never quite gets potent. And it is not for a lack of wanting to light this fire; it's that they don't quite know how.

This book is an attempt to change that and offer a match.

There is a profound connection between theological truth and your business interests. There is a wise way to grow a business, one that gets somewhere rather than running around in circles and taking you along for the ride. There is a way to grow in leadership, influence, and impact, from the time you are preparing to enter the business field all the way until the day before your funeral. There is a way to bypass the isolation, questioning, and deep frustration many face and instead, experience passion, purpose, fulfillment, and impact.

Leave the bulletins to someone else. You were created, redeemed, gifted, and enabled for so much more!

Letting Good Things Run Wild is divided into three major sections. The first is ***Deeper Faith***. Here, we will look at some of the theological doctrines that intimately apply to our business interests. This serves as a solid, bedrock foundation for us to build our business upon.

Next is a section called ***Better Business***. This is where we will explore a blueprint for developing and growing a business. Not just any business. Your business. Not just an average business. A better business. Better businesses are those that know what they are about, where they are going, exactly what they need, and have their organization rowing in the same direction. They are healthy, growing, and impactful. Sadly, they are also rare. But it is exactly the kind of business that yours can become.

The final section focuses on you: ***Greater Leadership Impact***. God has placed you in a unique environment to have a tremendous impact on others. We will look at the opportunities to mature and flourish in leadership roles that begin in your early years—before you even began your business—all the way into your latter days. We will look at how God takes you (all of us) through various growing and changing seasons of life and how leadership and influence cannot only grow deeper but also spread wider to impact a continually larger sphere of people.

So, why read this book? After all, there are numerous great books on theology. Amazon has thousands upon thousands of books on business. Probably the same for leadership. So again, why read this book? Because even though there are countless books on theology, business, and leadership, there are surprisingly few that show the intimate and powerful integration of all three. I want to provide you with a solid foundation upon which to grow and develop the most important business that you know. Yours!

Faith, business, and leadership are best implemented together. Take one of them out of your business equation, and the foundation for growth and impact becomes compromised. As Solomon wrote, "Though one may be overpowered, two can defend themselves, but a cord of three strands is not quickly broken" (Ecclesiastes 4:12). We hear this verse commonly used in wedding ceremonies because it's so vital to the strength, vitality, and success of the marriage relationship.

It is just as true for business.

Did you know that the triangle is the strongest and most stable geometric shape? The three sides provide an incredibly stable base, and shear forces are distributed throughout the entire shape making it exceptionally ridged. The triangle is the geometric shape of choice for architects because of this strength and stability.

Our businesses could stand to benefit from such properties.

The integration and interconnection of theology, business knowledge, and leadership provide for a great foundation. And foundations are meant to be built upon. With a proper understanding of the foundation, you will be able to sort through all of those numerous resources on theology, business, and leadership, and you will know how they specifically fit into the stewardship and thriving of your business.

Let's get started on connecting your faith with your business interests. It is a connection that will impact a great number of people. However, the one that will be impacted the most is *you*.

Let us explore how to build a deeper faith, better business, and greater impact. You will never regret doing things God's way. Take it from me: Your only regret will be waiting this long to do it.

GAINING A DEEPER FAITH THAT WILL IMPACT YOUR BUSINESS

The Grand Canyon is one of the most breathtaking sights in all of America. As it spans several states, there are areas where it's over one mile wide and other areas that are so deep, it would take you a couple of days of travel to get to the bottom. It is so big that every year, several people get lost in it. And every year, some of them are never found. It is indeed the biggest gap in the American landscape.

There are other gaps in America. They may not be as big, but a lot of people are getting lost in them. Spiritual truth that is given out on Sunday mornings at church may never make it to the workplace on Monday mornings. There is a huge gap that exists for too many people between Sunday and Monday. And too many things are getting lost.

What happens when a man can't connect real faith with 80 percent of his day? He's in a big hole.

What happens when a man understands the interconnection between real faith and his work? Some serious holes are filled up. And things are not getting lost anymore.

> *This is a trustworthy statement; and concerning these things I want you to speak confidently, so that those who have believed God will be careful to engage I good deeds. These things are good and profitable for men.*
> Titus 3:8

Chapter One

THE THEOLOGY OF WORK:
Starting Off on the Right Foundation

I stood before a group of guys, who had signed up to go through an eight-week series on the theology of work. I had taught this series every year for about fifteen years, and I always started out by asking the group a few questions.

"How many of you have ever heard a sermon series on the topic of work?"

No one raised his hand.

"How many of you at your church heard one good message entirely devoted to the topic of the workplace?"

Again, not one hand went up. And this scene was repeated over fifteen years.

It has been said that nature abhors a vacuum. Bad theology loves a vacuum since it will rush in and take over

3

to influence the thoughts, intentions, and actions of people because the truth has not been given a chance to even get into the fight. There are so many people of faith that share in some common views of the value of work. The problem is that even though they are very common views, they are also wrong.

And wrong theology has yet to produce anything of value for anyone.

Let's take a quick look at some of the common (yet wrong) views about the spiritual value of work.

Work Has No Spiritual Value

The view that work has no spiritual value comes from the belief that work is the result of the curse of sin found in Genesis 3. As a result, work is viewed as something negative and cursed. This view says work has no intrinsic value. No meaning or purpose. No real fulfillment or satisfaction. Work has become nothing more than a means to obtain a paycheck and some benefits. Work is something that must be endured until that blessed event when God will rapture his people out of the workplace and put them into that blissful state called retirement—where they will be free from the curse of work and can play for the rest of their days (yes, sarcasm is one of my love languages).

Work is the world of nine-to-five, Monday to Friday. The good life happens during the rest of the week. Work is seen as something that keeps us from the really important issues of life, like family and church. After all, that's what people are repeatedly told when they are at church.

Work is viewed as something greedy, corrupting, sinful, and competitive. It has no spiritual value at all.

Work Has False Spiritual Value

This common view of work affirms that work has a great deal of value. However, it's the wrong kind of value. Instead of being godly or righteous, it is really idolatry. And it's deadly.

This view of work believes that work is what gives us our identity, power, and wealth. "Work is what will make me a success." When left unchecked, this leads its followers into putting work on a pedestal, and it becomes the idol to which they bow down and give their allegiance.

Let's take a quick look at Isaiah 44:12–15, where the prophet talks about some of the craftsmen of his day.

The man shapes iron into a cutting tool, and does his work over the coals, fashioning it with hammers, and working it with his strong arm. He also gets hungry, and his strength fails; he drinks no water and becomes weary. Another shapes wood, he extends a measuring line; he outlines it with red chalk. He works it with planes, and outlines it with a compass, and makes it like the form of a man, like the beauty of man, so that it may sit in a house. Surely, he cuts cedars for himself, and takes a cypress or an oak, and raised it for himself among the trees of the forest. He plants a fir, and the rain makes it grow (Isaiah 44:12–14).

This guy is a blue-collar laborer and is working hard. He doesn't even stop for a drink of water. He is outfitted like a guy that might be on a Lowe's commercial. He is skilled. People are buying his craftwork to place in their homes. He is even planting more trees for future inventory, sales, and growth. Isaiah is showing us this common business model, and it looks impressive. But now, Isaiah gives us a view of what is going on at the heart level and what is going on deep inside.

> *Then it becomes something for a man to burn, so he takes on of them and warms himself; he also makes a fire to bake bread. He also makes a god and worships it; he makes it a graven image and falls down before it. Half of it he burns in the fire; over this half, he eats meat as he roasts a roast and is satisfied. He also warms himself and says, "Aha! I am warm, I have seen the fire". But the rest of it he makes into a god, his graven image, he falls down before it and worships; he also prays to it and says, "Deliver me, for thou art my God" (Isaiah 44:15–17).*

He has busted his butt at work so that he can enjoy the fruit of his labors. Now inside his home, he has a warm fire. Bread is baking. For crying out loud, he has an entire roast on the fire that he is preparing to eat! No microwave meal for this dude. All this is courtesy of a fire made from some of the wood from his business. He uses part of a log to warm his home and serve his desires . . . and from the other half, he carves out an idol, worships it, and prays that it would be his deliverer.

We can look at this passage and shrug off the message, believing this is about pagans living hundreds of years ago.

Bowing before idols of wood and stone is so "Old Testament" and not applicable to our modern and sophisticated times.

Theologians often refer to this as "chronological snobbery." Others call it being stupid.

Remove the wood and replace it with a career. Or a job title. Or an office suite with all the authority that comes with it. Many are still placing their innermost allegiance to those things that bring them comfort: identity, power, and wealth. It's the same idolatry. It's just wearing a different jersey.

What happens to many that cling to this false view of work is that they wind up rather empty. The payoff for all the hard work, sacrifice, time, and energy is promised to be there at the next level. But when the next level is reached, the satisfaction is like cotton candy. It's gone soon after the first bite and only a fleeting sugar rush remains. After achieving all that they have been striving for, they are left with this gnawing question: "Is that all that there is to this life?"

Work Has Limited Spiritual Value

That work has limited spiritual value is probably the most common view of work in the evangelical church. Even though it is common, it does not mean that it is correct. This view believes that work is part of the *secular* world and should not be confused with the *sacred* world. Here, work can have some value *if*:

- work is done for a church or ministry of some sort
- work is a place for evangelizing the lost

- work is viewed as a source to donate time or money to help keep the church or ministry in the black

This view believes it is more spiritual to be the church secretary than a receptionist at the doctor's office. That coordinating the summer Vacation Bible School is more righteous than teaching the fourth-grade classroom during the school year. Or one might even hear the common declaration, "I can't wait to retire because then I will be able to serve God!" from someone who accepts this view.

This common belief holds that there are secular kinds of work and sacred kinds of work and that the primary difference is found in *what kind* of occupation or work you are involved in.

However, the Scriptures say very little, if anything, about secular and sacred jobs but say a great deal about *why* we do the work we do. Is the work being done as unto the Lord, or is it not?

It is estimated that about 2–3 percent of the people in our church congregations wind up in some type of vocational ministry. And make no mistake about it, these people fill vital roles that allow good ministry to get done. But what about the other 97 percent that does not go into these occupations? Are these people destined to live most of their waking hours sitting on the "secular" bench while a chosen few get to do the important "sacred" work? One of the problems with this flawed view of work is that it doesn't just affect the workplace. It tends to spread.

British essayist and author Dorothy Sayers nailed it when she wrote, "If we no longer see work as sacred, is it no wonder that we no longer see faith as sacred? After all, who could be interested in a religion that has no connection with nine-tenths of life?"

That will preach, sister!

Let me ask you this: is there a disconnect between God and your work? Is there somewhere in your life where a great chasm exists between Sunday and Monday, where spiritual truth seems to get lost? Unfortunately, this is the most common experience for people of faith in the marketplace. The result is many people having work without meaning . . . tasks without purpose, projects without fulfillment, and life without passion.

Has any of these thoughts crossed your mind:

- "I need my work to have more meaning."
- "I need a clear picture of what being a person of faith on the job really looks like."
- "I want a faith that makes a real difference in my job and in my life."
- "I am tired of juggling two different worlds and trying to make sense of how they connect."
- "I feel that I am not receiving any help to bring these two worlds together."

Can I offer some encouragement? If you have looked at any of these statements and thought, "Yep, that's me!" then your world is about to get rocked. Psalm 31:3 declares, "For you are my rock and my fortress. For your name's sake You will lead me and guide me" (NASB). God's Word will lead us to a deep and fulfilling reality of how He is intimately and intentionally connected to our business interests. He is the Rock that we can, and should, build our business interests on.

We will see that:

- Work is ordained by God
- You were created by God to work
- There is a deep, profound, and highly significant connection between you…God…and your work.

There can exist a seamless connection between Sunday and Monday. And from Monday to Sunday. It is a seamless life built upon the God of communion . . . and the workplace. The Lord of the Bible study . . . and your business meetings. The Creator of the heavens and the earth . . . and your job. Wearing the shoes of the gospel of peace along with your best business suit or work clothes—it is all intimately connected.

And the Truth Will Set You Free!

God places a high value on work. In fact, He is very big on this as we can see in the first pages of the Scriptures. In Genesis 1 and 2, we see the following:

- God was working. He was creating everything out of nothing.
- God also created man and immediately, we see that God gave the man some work to do.
- While God was creating everything, He was doing it all by Himself.

- Yet, God was intimately involved in all the work the man was given to accomplish.

If you were to describe God in these first two chapters, how would you describe Him? Powerful? Eternal? Creator? These are all very accurate and true indeed. But how about "Worker?"

I think for many of us, we sometimes get caught up in the common theological trees, and we miss the obvious forest. God is powerful and eternal. God is the One true Creator of all. These are all part of His incredible nature. So is working. Work is also woven into the character of mankind as part of His creation. God declared, "Let Us make man in Our image, according to Our likeness . . . and God created man in His own image, in the image of God He created him; male and female He created them."

What was a dominant image or likeness of God that we see in these early pages of scripture? He's a worker.

What is one of the dominant things that we see the man doing in the garden? That's right, working. He's naming animals. He's been instructed by God to "tend and keep" the garden. God even instructs the first couple with a command to continue with this work when He declared, "Be fruitful and multiply, and fill the earth, and subdue it; and rule over the fish of the sea and over the birds of the sky, and over every living thing that moves on the earth" (Genesis 1:28). This isn't just a command to have more kids (although having nine children of my own, I highly recommend it!), but it's also a command to create, to work, and to move out and expand. Theologians often refer to this as the "Creation Mandate." It can also be man's first job description.

We can observe and learn so much from these first two chapters of Scripture. They contain a deep, deep river of truth, principles, insights, and things for us to understand. One of them is the tremendous value that God places upon work. It's seen in His nature and actions. It is seen in man's nature and actions. It is seen in the commands and marching orders that God gives to mankind.

And notice that all of this occurred before sin entered the picture and screwed it all up.

The Big Three

When I say, "The Big Three," you are probably thinking about the Trinitarian nature of God. Good for you. However, I want to draw our attention to the three institutions that God intentionally created in these early chapters of Genesis. They are marriage, parenting, and (drum roll, please) *work*. All of these were created before the Fall. They are all good, valuable, delightful, and purposeful. They were given to man to enjoy and in their proper expression, they give honor and glory to God. This is by God's design.

Then comes Chapter Three. Selfishness, pride, and an enemy appear, and all hell breaks loose. We know from Scripture—and our own life experience—that sin affects *everything*. All of Creation has now become a broken, dysfunctional image of what God created. When man rebelled and sinned, and God showed up on the scene, He declared what the fallout would be.

Now, since sin does affect everyone and everything, God could have used so many numerous examples to tell us how things were going to be moving forward. But look at the specific issues He chose to use:

"To the woman He said, 'I will greatly multiply your pain in childbirth, and in pain you shall bring forth children'" (Genesis 3:16, NASB). Mothers are intimately aware of the pain in childbirth. Thank God for epidurals! But the term "bring forth" does not refer to the birthing process, but rather, the process of raising our children. That is also going to be painful. Parenting will have its time of sorrow and hardship.

"Yet your desire shall be for your husband, and he shall rule over you" (Gen. 3:16b, RSV). This is His declaration that the marriage relationship will now have to contend with conflict. These words desire and rule are not healthy at all. These suggest that there will be a fight to be first in the marriage relationship and to control the spouse. Not good at all. Yet, it's as common as the sun coming up in the morning.

"Cursed is the ground . . . thorns and thistles it shall grow for you . . . eat plants . . . sweat on your face . . . and then return to the dust" (Genesis 3:17b–19). Work has been cursed as well.

Parenting. Marriage. Work. All given to man to enjoy. All specifically pointed out by God for us to understand that sin infects and affects everything. All are institutions highly valued by God. In fact, if you look in the book of Ephesians, in Chapters 5 and 6, you will see a familiar pattern, only now it's about God redeeming what sin has broken. The apostle Paul writes about our need to be filled with the Spirit (5:18) and then what Spirit-filled relationships should look like (5:22–6:9). What examples of Spirit-filled relationships are given? Where might God want to show off His power of redemption, transformation, and salvation?

Marriage, parenting, and work.

What sin has broken and destroyed, God wants to redeem and make whole. His plans for mankind still involve the institutions of marriage, parenting, and work. It is important for us to realize this because it appears that God really puts a high value on these institutions. So, why is it that so many people of faith take their theology from the great prophet Meat Loaf, who encouraged many to believe that two out of three ain't bad? We often treat marriage and parenting as the two favorite daughters in the home, and work is the ugly stepchild of the family.

This is why we find so many incorrect ideas about the spiritual value of work. Yes, work is broken. Yes, work is hard. Yes, we find greed, corruption, and selfishness. But we also have a divorce rate hovering around 50 percent and so many struggling marriages that when a couple announces they are engaged to get married, it's hard to know whether to say "Congratulations!" or "I'm so sorry to hear that." When a couple announces they are expecting their firstborn, we don't mourn and tell them all they can expect is a world of hurt. No, we honor marriage. We celebrate children. This is because God created these institutions with dignity and value to honor Him and benefit mankind.

It's about time we give work the dignity and value it deserves.

Once we, as individuals, come to understand this theological reality and embrace it with all of our hearts, souls, minds, and strength, the impact can be powerful.

And Monday is gonna look a whole lot better!

A family traveled to the New England area to visit relatives. On Sunday morning, they attended the local church and sat down in the front pew with the little girl sitting next to her mother. This church was typical of many of the older churches in the area. Ornate in its décor. Wood craftsmanship throughout. A huge organ for music and a balcony area for overflow seating. And an impressive three-sided pulpit at center stage. It was one of those pulpits that had a few steps inside that the preacher climbed up to look over the congregation. As the preacher moved into his message, his voice began to grow louder.

Preachers like to refer to this as "making a point."

As the little girl listened to the preacher talking louder, she started to sink down in the pew and asked her mother, "What is he doing?"

"He's preaching, Sweetie."

The preacher continued to speak louder and louder as he moved through his message. We preachers like to refer to this as "speaking with authority." Really, it's just being excited and starting to yell.

The little girl, now getting a little frightened by the man in the big box on the stage yelling at people, turned to her mother and asked, "What happens if he gets out of the box?"

What happens when we connect our faith in Him to our business interests?

We get out of the box and let good things run wild.

Chapter Two

CALLING

Then the LORD God took the man and put him into the garden . . .

Genesis 2:15a

N ow that we have seen that God does indeed place a high value on the institution of work, let's look at some of the blocks that make up this theological foundation for us to build upon. We are going to start by looking at the doctrine of *calling* and how vital it is in our business interest. There can be a powerful dynamic when a career is united with a calling.

The word *career* finds its origin in the Latin word *carrus,* which means "wheeled vehicle." This was usually a cart or chariot that was used to transport people or heavy loads. In the sixteenth century, the French and Italian languages picked up on the word and used it to denote a road or racecourse. The verb form of the word was used to denote running at a high speed. So, the word *career* originally described pushing or pulling a cart around a racetrack as fast as you could.

Right now, some of you are thinking, "Yep, you just described my job!" Not much has changed for hundreds of years.

A *calling* is altogether different. A calling is linear. It is a trajectory. It is going somewhere that is strategic, intentional, and loaded with purpose.

A career without the context of a calling is something that can be described as riding a bicycle around a cul-de-sac at the end of a road. Bob gets up every morning and hops on the latest and greatest of customized road bikes to begin his workday. He checks his state-of-the-art smartwatch and logs onto the fitness app. And then he peddles his brains out. Riding hard, he checks the numerous metrics on his watch as the day unfolds. At the end of the day, Bob compares the day's metrics against past performances and evaluates his progress toward meeting the monthly, quarterly, and yearly goals that have been set for bike riding.

When Bob finishes his day of riding, he smiles as he evaluates all the goals he has accomplished and all the work he has done. Then he gets off his bike at the same place in the cul-de-sac where he started that morning. And the same place he will start tomorrow. And the year after that as well. Except that Bob will have a new list of goals to accomplish. Pushing his cart around the track as fast as he can.

Pushing hard. Accomplishing goals. Lots of activity without any real progress.

Is working hard wrong? Not at all. In fact, it's a noble characteristic that should be embraced. Is it OK to set goals to monitor progress and achievement? Again, yes. But we should derive our goals out of our calling. Our calling is what drives us, and our goals are set to help us accomplish it. However, when your goals are the dominant and driving force in your life, what happens when you get to the point where you accomplish all of your goals? You now have lost your reason for living.

Bob has traded in his yearly upgraded bike riding in the cul-de-sac for being the lion in the zoo. Our family visited a lot of zoos when our kids were younger. I remember one of my sons was most eager to see the lions and tigers. The big cats. The King of the jungle. You can imagine his disappointment when all he saw were large, powerful lions just lying around all day, looking around and occasionally yawning.

He asked me what was wrong with them. I wanted to say that this is what happens to an executive who spends most of his life being driven by goals and then finds himself near the end of his career or even retired. But I didn't think a four-year-old would quite understand, so I told him that living in a cage is not what lions were created to do, and this is what happens to them. No real living. No passion. Nothing left to live for except eat, yawn, nap, and wait to die.

This is the result of the goal-driven, cul-de-sac-riding, career-*without-calling* life explained to a four-year-old.

Many people of faith have some difficulty connecting calling with their careers, but they can (and should!) fit together quite nicely. Think of it this way:

A career is what you are *paid* to do.
A calling is what you are *made* to do.
And when the two become one flesh,
it's a beautiful thing to behold!

Chocolate is great. Peanut butter is wonderful. But when the two become united as one . . . that's a treat that can be enjoyed for all the days of your life!

The Theology of Calling

Calling is not something that is reserved for only certain people of faith that have attained some special status or place in God's eyes. Calling is a reality for every person of faith that has a relationship with God through Christ. There are three callings from God that we experience.

First, God calls us to Himself for our salvation. We didn't earn our salvation; He gives it. We don't first seek out God; He seeks us out. He calls us, and we have the opportunity to answer the phone.

Then, God calls His people of faith into a two-fold mission. One aspect of that mission is that He is continually working in us throughout our lifetimes with the goal of conforming us into the image of His Son (Romans 8:28–30). The other part of this calling is that He calls us to *do* something.

One is the call to *being*. The other is the call to *doing*. One is what God is doing on the inside of us. The other is the expression of our faith to others through our actions . . . and work. Both callings are working themselves throughout our lives in an ongoing dynamic of internal growth manifested in external tasks and missions. As we look at this calling to being/doing in the Scriptures, there appears to be a common theme. God works on our inner man to cause us to grow deeper in our faith, character, and maturity. Times of trial or hardship. Seasons of quiet and stillness. Periods of pressure and squeezing. All these things He is working together to bring us a more strengthened character. Then comes the doing. A project to do. A task to accomplish. A mission to fulfill. A place or people to impact.

Look at the life of Joseph in Genesis. Or Moses, David, or Abraham in the Old Testament. Or Peter and Paul in Acts. There is a pattern where God prepared them before He used them. He wanted them to be strong in character so they would not collapse under the weight of what tasks God was calling them to do. When character is lacking, it doesn't take very much weight of responsibility to bring it all crashing down. And the damage can be devastating.

Steven Berglas, a psychologist at Harvard Medical School and author of *The Success Syndrome*, writes that people who achieve great heights but lack the bedrock character to sustain them through the pressure and stress that often come with those achievements are headed for disaster. He believes they are destined for one or more of the four *A*s: arrogance, painful feelings of aloneness, destructive adventure-seeking, or adultery. Each of these by itself is a terrible price to pay for a weak character. Some experience more than one. The one group that seems to touch all four bases are televangelists. It's another reminder that even though God may have chosen us, we can still choose stupid all on our own. The understanding of the reality of calling can help keep us off the casualty list.

So, we see that God does call individuals to Himself for salvation and the beginning of a relationship with Him. We also see that those whom God has called to Himself, He is also calling them to become more into the image of His Son. So, let's dive into this third aspect of calling: being called to do something.

Here is a simple working definition of what this calling looks like. Calling can be thought of as:

**A message from God to you,
concerning a task, project, endeavor, or mission,
to a certain target audience or group,
for a desired impact or result that honors God,
benefits them, and greatly satisfies you.**

Let's break this down so that we can better understand the great value that calling brings to people of faith in the marketplace.

First, calling is a message from God to you. That's right . . . YOU. Calling is highly personal. As people of faith, we have a *relationship* with the one true God. He tells us that He wants to be known as our heavenly *Father*. When God makes a person, it's highly personal! Psalm 139 says that when He made us, we were "fearfully and wonderfully made." That translates as being "made with reverence" and "to be made with distinction." When He made you, it was not as some mass-produced product that is high-quantity and low-value. Nope. You were made with great *reverence*. That's a work of great art rather than a paint-by-numbers creation. You are also made with *distinction*. That means a work that is intentional, strategic, thought-out, planned, and made for a purpose.

Why do you love to take risks, create jobs for others, and see opportunities that many others just don't see? Because you were made that way. Why does the knowledge of how the human body works fascinate you, and the sight of blood and guts doesn't gross you out, but rather, you find it kind of cool? What makes you want to fix people, helping them get better? Could it be that a huge part of that is because you were intentionally made that way? Why can you build a house, balance a ledger, counsel the hurting, deliver a service, or lead a team? Because you were fearfully and wonderfully made to do these things! Embrace the gifts, talents, and skills that you have and at the same time, embrace the One who gave you these things. They were given to you so that you could use them for a purpose, one that God calls you to be part of.

The concept of calling in the business world is vital, but it has also been greatly cheapened over the years. There are many people who talk about their "calling" into various ventures. There are numerous business/life/executive coaches—along with books, seminars, and speakers—that encourage people to live out their "calling." But there seems to be something extremely critical that is missing.

Who is Doing the Calling?

If someone has a *calling*, then it implies that someone is the *caller*. If you cannot identify who is calling you, then you are just talking to yourself. You are also deceiving yourself. Talking to yourself, listening to yourself, and then dressing it up as your "calling" makes it sound impressive, but it's really just selfishness. Talking to God and listening to Him and then acting on your calling does sound impressive . . . because it really is!

God made you on purpose, and He will lead you into those purposes. For most of you reading this, you may find those skills, talent, gifts, and desires expressed primarily in the marketplace.

And it's time that many of you embrace His calling with a greater and clearer assurance you are God's workmanship created for the good works that He has prepared for you.

Second, is the idea that God's calling for you concerns a specific task, project, endeavor, or mission. You cannot solve all the problems in the world—or in your community. But you can be the solution to a specific problem or need. You are not all of God's program, but you are certainly part of the team. You are part of God's solution for a world in need. As we talked about before, you have been given certain gifts, talent, skills, abilities, and desires to meet certain needs of others.

When you realize that your specific business interests result from you responding to what God is calling you to do, it brings the necessary clarity to you and your organization. To be able to understand and communicate with confidence, "This is who we are. This is what we do. This is what we are about. This is where we are headed . . ." is a powerful foundation in a successful business. It gets everyone rowing in the same direction.

Third, calling is a message from God to you concerning a certain task that impacts a specific group or audience. We're talking about the customer to be served. The group to hear your talk. The group that needs to be poured into to grow and get better. Somewhere along the line of your work efforts, there are people. It involves your customers, patients, students, staff, direct reports, vendors, or clients. There may be a small number of them or a multitude. Either way, God has called you into a place where He is working in you and through you to get to them.

Last, there is a desired impact that happens. You were created by God, redeemed by God, and then called by God to go to work with God to have an impact on people. Who would not want that in their job description! In fact, let's take a look at what this might look like in your business.

What if, deep in your soul, you understood that the work of your hands and the decisions that you made within your business truly honored God? That you were working in a way that God designed and created you for? That at the end of your workday, God would be saying, "Well done good and faithful servant" (Matthew 25:23, NIV).

What if people were really benefiting from the results of your work and business efforts? That their lives would somehow be better because they purchased your product, paid for your service, or were employed by your business? What if people benefited so much from your business efforts that should your business suddenly come to an end, they would mourn, and some might even weep?

What if all of this was true of you and your business? That God is truly honored by your business. That other people are significantly benefited from your business. When you think that all of this is not some false fairy tale but is a reality for those who embrace His calling into the marketplace, then a deep personal fulfillment and satisfaction are what emerges. That's something of great significance. That's a clear and passionate focus. That's a profound purpose.

Imagine what it is like to put your head on a pillow at night after living a day like that at work. Imagine waking up the next morning to do it all again. Only better this time.

That's the incredible and powerful reality of calling, as we connect our personal faith with our business interests.

Chapter Three
STEWARDSHIP

Then the LORD God took the man and put him into the garden of Eden to cultivate and keep it.
Genesis 2:15

When you hear the word *stewardship*, what comes to mind? Be honest—what are the first thoughts that come into your head? I think for most people of faith, they think back to times at church where calls for "being good stewards" are heard while offering plates are being passed. Or those special days that are referred to as "Stewardship Sundays," which means you will be encouraged to write an even bigger check (remember, I have been part of a pastoral team for almost two decades, so I'm talking about the team on my side of the ball). Or, when we hear our friends (or even ourselves) saying that they just "want to be a good steward of God's resources" when they are considering a significant purchase of an item. Translation: "I want to spend as little as possible on this."

For most of us, we view stewardship with giving. That's not wrong because stewardship does involve giving resources to others. But in reality, it's a whole lot more than just giving. And it's a whole lot more exciting to live it!

To help us understand the magnificence of stewardship we are going to look at two parables that offer us insight into the richness of stewardship.

The Parable of the Cereal Aisle

We have some friends that were well into the years of raising their house full of kids when an opportunity came up to adopt a baby. The little guy (let's call him Stevie) had some significant health issues—one of which caused him to need around-the-clock oxygen. As a result, Stevie did not leave the house until his body got stronger. Introducing foods to Stevie was a slow process, but eventually, he found his favorite food: Cheerios. Stevie loved breakfast and breakfast meant cereal, and there was only one cereal in the house—Cheerios.

At about four years of age, Stevie was able to take short trips out of the house. One day, he had his first trip to the grocery store. He was riding high in the cart and enjoying the new sights. And then it happened. The cart turned down the cereal aisle.

Stevie knew then that Heaven must be real.

Rows upon rows of cereal stretching all the way down to the end of the aisle! All kinds of cereal! Granola, Captain Crunch, Fruit Loops, and Frosted Flakes. Fruity Pebbles and Cocoa Puffs! And not only Cheerios, but all kinds of Cheerios: Honey Nut, Multi-Grain, Frosted, and others he had no ideas even existed.

Stevie's joy was indeed full because he now realized that cereal is more than just Cheerios.

The same can be said of stewardship. When God calls us to breakfast, He's offering a whole lot more than just Cheerios.

The Parable of the Talents

This parable is found in Matthew 25, and it is part of a group of parables that Jesus told to his disciples to answer their question, "Tell us, when will these things be, and what will be the sign of Your coming, and of the end of the age?" He laid out three parables with messages in response to their questions.

- The parable of the Fig Tree: the signs of when He is near.
- The parable of the Ten Virgins: wait expectantly for Him.
- The parable of the Talents: while we are waiting for Him, we should work exceptionally with Him.

So what does it mean "to work exceptionally with Jesus" until He comes?

**It means that we should invest
time in church and Bible study!**
*(Sure, but what about the time when
we are not in church or a Bible study?)*

**It means that we should be
intentional about sharing the gospel!**
*(Absolutely, but what about the other
conversations when we are not sharing the gospel?)*

**It means that we should be giving
generously to the local church and missionaries!**
(Yeah, but what about the rest of our time, money, and resources?)

There is something more than Cheerios going on in the world of stewardship, and when we begin to understand it, then life becomes a long, long aisle full of choices and opportunities to explore!

So, grab a spoon, and let's dig in!

For it is just like a man about to go on a journey, who called his own slaves, and entrusted his possessions to them (v.14).

Stewardship is something highly relational. This verse references a very wealthy landowner. He was about to embark on a business trip, so he called a few of his servants to him. Notice that he only called a few of them. Not all of them . . .

just a few. These were handpicked by the master. In fact, it says they were *called* (see the previous chapter in case you forgot it already). This is not arbitrary. This is personal. This is highly relational. This is the reality of stewardship!

Stewardship is a vital expression of our calling from our Master. Notice how deeply personal this is. The master *entrusts* his own possessions to these servants. Trust is something that we give to others because we know them. The more we know them, the more we trust them, and the more we can entrust to them. God entrusts things to you out of His relationship with you. You were chosen by Him so that you can know Him, and He wants to entrust things to you.

What did the master entrust to his servants? His possessions. We will see in a little bit that what this guy possessed was *huge*! He owned an incredible agricultural enterprise with land that covered a few zip codes, livestock galore, crops as far as the eye could see, and a huge staff to take care of it all. These were his possessions. These were the things that he entrusted to the few servants he called to his side. That's a whole lot of stuff. That's a whole lot of trust. That's the picture of real, loyal, and deeply significant relationships.

What has God entrusted to you? Think about your business. Who are the people that are part of your business (employees, vendors, clients, customers, patients, etc.)? What are the resources that are part of your business? The facilities, equipment, inventory, bank accounts, cash? What about the opportunities that have come your way? Expansion, growth, merger, relocation, product lines, networks? All those people . . . all these opportunities . . . and all these resources that God has entrusted to *you*. He did not entrust them to someone else, but He specifically and intentionally called you to Himself and entrusted all of this to you.

> *And to one he gave five talents, to another, two and to another, one, each according to his own ability; and he went on his journey (v.15).*

Before he left on his business trip, this businessman entrusted to these three servants something called a *talent*. Now, a talent in this context is not referring to the ability to sing in the choir, play the piano, or organize the children's ministry. Those certainly are skills and really valuable, but the word *talent* here refers to a unit of measure. A talent was a measure of two hundred pounds of something—usually silver or gold. The higher the value of the transaction, the more likely gold was the item to be weighed. If one was to give an estimate or best guess on the value of something, they would use a talent as twenty years of wages—a significant amount of money.

Let's put this into today's context. Currently, the price of gold in the US is $1,708 per ounce. That translates to $27,328 per pound. That makes the value of a talent in today's market $5,465,600. I think the word *talent* comes from a Greek word meaning, "that's a whole lot of jack!"

So, one servant gets five talents (over $27M), another gets two talents (almost $11M), and another gets one talent (about $5.5M). The owner is not just handing out bonuses here; he is entrusting these specific amounts to these specific servants *according to their abilities*. Again, this is not a random act of distribution of assets. It is intentional. Thought through. Well planned.

Have you ever considered that God created you with specific talents, abilities, skills, and desires so that He can entrust something of tremendous value to you? Could it be that He created you and placed you in the position you find yourself in regarding your business or corporation? Is it a stretch to think that in the sovereignty of God, He created you intentionally to have the abilities to lead the business you oversee with all the people, opportunities, and resources, which may be valued in the millions?

That's not a stretch. That's connecting dots.

That's God . . . and you . . . and stewardship. Ready for another spoonful?

Immediately, the one who had received the five talents went and traded with them and gained five more. In the same manner, the one who had received two talents gained two more (v. 16–17).

Did you notice what they did once they received their talents? They *immediately* went out and started trading with it. Why? Because that is what the master wanted them to do with it. Not just watch over it. Not be foolish with it. Not spend it all on themselves as if it was their reward for faithful service. They traded with it. Engaged in business with it. They went out and did this immediately and passionately, just as they were trained by their boss to do. This was no half-hearted effort on their part. The results of their business plan yielded significant results. The one with five now had ten. The one with two now had four. That's 100 percent growth of the investment! This is a significant part of what stewardship is. If there is one word that is synonymous with stewardship it is this: GROWTH.

This falls right in line with my favorite verse concerning personal and time management.

Therefore, be careful how you walk, not as unwise men, but as wise, making the most of your time because the days are evil (Ephesians 5:15–16).

Paul says the days are evil (you aren't kidding!), and as part of living as wise people, we should make the most of our time. Who's time? Your time. Not others', not a group's, but your time. And we are instructed to make the *most* of it. Making is creating, developing, building, and developing. Most implies something better or greater. It's growing something to be as good as it can get. This is the admonition to get off our blessed assurance and, in the words of that great theologian, Larry the Cable Guy, "Let's get 'er done!"

However, not every steward on the ranch wants to join in on the adventure. There are those who prefer to go rogue and pursue their own plans.

But he who received the one talent went away and dug in the ground, and hid his master's money (v.18).

Stewardship can have all sorts of variance. Some are entrusted with five talents, others with two. Some have one business, others have multiple. Some oversee gross sales in six figures, others see millions and more. But one thing is consistent with stewardship in every person: it will reveal your heart.

No matter how much you have or how little you have, how you choose to take care of what has been entrusted to you is a clear expression of what is going on inside of you for others to see. That's what work does. That's what money does. These things are not morally good or morally bad. But they are definitely revealing.

Why do you think this third servant chose to put the $5.5M into a hidden account? He does provide his line of reasoning later in the chapter. Personally, I don't buy it because the master certainly didn't buy his excuses. I think he hid the money because he probably thought the master might not make it back, and if the master doesn't come back, then the money is all his. Go ahead and read to the end of the parable. It did not end well for him. Visions that only serve to benefit ourselves usually don't end well.

So, what is your vision for making the most of the people, opportunities, and resources that have been entrusted to you by God, according to your abilities? Do you realize that it is not only a good idea to grow your business interests but when a heart has declared allegiance to God, that growth may well be a righteous desire and objective?

Now, some may say that the desire for the growth of one's business interests is greedy, selfish, and corrupt. They certainly are right. We see it everywhere. However, those people of faith that sincerely desire to connect their faith with their business interests have a different set of marching orders. It's found all the way back in the beginning when God told the first couple to be fruitful and multiply; fill the earth and subdue it; rule over it. Take what has been given to you and expand it with the abilities that you have been given. Make the most of it. It's what you have been called to do!

Now after a long time the master of those slaves came and settled accounts with them (v. 19).

The master finally returned from his business trip, and it does say that he was gone for quite a while. Upon returning, it was time for a staff meeting to turn in some reports to see what progress was made while he was gone. We see that the one who had five created five more, and the one who had two, created two more. Look at what the master said to both because of the responsible growth they produced.

Well done, good and faithful servant; you were faithful with a few things, I will put you in charge of many things, enter into the joy of your master (vs. 21,23).

They were described as good and faithful. Not a bad review from the boss. They were also given some increasing responsibilities, and they were able to enter a relational experience described as joy. I am not endorsing the prosperity gospel that believes that faithfulness will always result in more wealth, prosperity, and even private jets. Nor am I suggesting that people of faith have nothing but rainbows and balloons and all-day happiness at work. The reality of the curse of sin on work is something that we all know all too well. But joy is something that people of faith can experience at work. Joy is something that has depth, strength, and staying power. It's one of the advantages that people of faith have in the business world when they realize that God created them with distinction and called them into the business world to make the most of the people, opportunities, and resources that have been entrusted to them.

Would you allow me a bit of theological speculation? I often wonder what would have happened if the master in the parable stayed away even longer than he had? What if the good and faithful servants were given even more time to make the most of their talents? I think the one who was given five talents may have been able to produce seven more. Maybe the one given two would have produced three or four more? I tend to think so because the servants faithfully worked until the master came and told them to stop. Then, he called them to some new or greater responsibilities. That is the heart of a good and faithful steward: create the most out of the people, opportunities, and resources to honor the Master and benefit others . . . and that their own joy may be full.

And then do it again tomorrow. And the next day. And the day after that.

Someday, God will call an end to your season of work and business. It may be a time to hand it off to another, or it may be that you are standing face to face with Him. Until that time arrives, you have the privilege to embrace stewardship in your business interests. Remember, stewardship is more than just giving away time, finances, and resources—even as important as those things are. Giving is a joy to experience and Cheerios are really good for breakfast. But there is a whole aisle of things to enjoy for those who deeply connect their faith with their business interests.

Grab a big spoon and enjoy growing all that God has entrusted to you.

Chapter Four

CHARACTER AND INTEGRITY
IN THE MARKETPLACE

And out of the ground the LORD God caused to grow
every tree that is pleasing to the sight and good for food:
the tree of the life also in the midst of the garden, and the
tree of the knowledge of good and evil.
Genesis 2:9

There is quite a bit of talk concerning the issues of character
and integrity in the workplace. Most would agree these are
important qualities to have as a business leader, and as everyone
nods their head in agreement, it's time to move on to other
issues at hand. After all, there is work that needs to be done.
Nothing to see here folks. Let's keep things moving along in

the right direction. The truth is that there is quite a bit to be seen here, folks. And it is worth our time and attention to stop and take a good, hard look at character and integrity in the workplace. Specifically, *your* character and integrity.

Character and integrity can be thought of as colors of various shades and hues. They fill in the lines of the picture of our work and bring out a distinctiveness in our work.

Give a three-year-old a picture from a coloring book and a set of crayons and tell him to color the picture. There is a cute picture of a puppy playing in the yard, and Timmy grabs a purple crayon and scribbles all over the page. Then, as an extra measure of artistic flair, he grabs a brown crayon and adds some more scribbles over other areas of the drawing. Then Mom takes the picture of the purple grass, flowers, puppy, and everything else and places it on the refrigerator door to display for all to see.

When people see the purple puppy and the brown sky, they draw some conclusions:

"This is so cute!" (The mom has to say this because it is her kid after all.)

What happened to the other sixty-four colors in the crayon box?

Timmy thinks that the black outlines and shapes in the picture are nothing more than suggestions because staying within them is something out of his control.

Because this reveals the inner workings of a three-year-old, we say it is cute. If it is the work of the forty-year-old father who runs a business and is responsible to lead others, well . . . we call this tragic.

Now, let's say that Mama wants to put a picture on the refrigerator door, as well. Only mama has taken a page out of one of those adult-level coloring books. The picture is incredibly detailed with its shapes and designs. All that it lacks is color. Mama takes a set of eighty-eight fine-point markers and with patience, skill, and time, colors in the page. This is also on display for all to see. Your eyes are drawn to it. It captures your attention and imagination. You see beauty, creativity, and wonder.

This reflects what is inside Mama being made manifest to the outside world.

The same can be said of character and integrity.

And it does not matter if your inner character and integrity are like the mother or the three-year-old; either way, it will be on display for others to see. So, it's foolish for us to move swiftly on from this topic thinking there is "nothing to see here, folks . . . keep moving along."

Because there is a lot for everyone to see.

Character and Integrity: What is it?

Integrity is more than being a nice person or doing the right thing for the right reason, at the right time. Integrity refers to the wholeness or authenticity of something. An *integer* is a whole number. If something is *integral* it is an essential part that makes something whole. Integrity is often used to describe the quality of wood. If you cut down a tree and look at the inside and see that it has uniform color—solid density starting at the center and extending all the way to the bark—you would say the wood within the tree has good integrity. If the inside is overly dry, filled with holes, and has bugs crawling around, then the wood has poor integrity.

Near my home is a community called the Amana Villages. Steeped in an old German heritage, this village has several shops showcasing rich German traditions and customs. My favorite is the furniture store. Here you can find some of the most incredible, hand-crafted pieces of furniture that radiate quality, craftsmanship, and excellence. My favorite is the roll-top desks. These desks are only built through a customized order and take a few years to finally reach completion. Pure furniture heaven!

We also have a major university in our backyard, and with it comes a multitude of students needing furnishings for their dorm room. The local Walmart and Target stores sell a huge number of desks to the students. They usually run under $100, and some may last throughout the school year. If you cut into these desks, you would primarily see a cheap fiberboard with a slick-looking wood veneer on the outside. Pure furniture cheapness!

Integrity can certainly describe wood.

It can also describe a person.

I'm sure that several faces and names are coming to you right now. Those who you would describe as solid, genuine, whole, or healthy . . . as well as those who are nothing more than filler on the inside trying to hide behind a flashy veneer.

Character is a term that originally referred to an engraving instrument that was used by an artisan. The tool was used to make certain distinctive marks that would give the artwork individuality and uniqueness. Character is a collection of individual choices and actions that create a portrait of who you really are.

Let's do a little deep dive into a few essential attributes of good character and integrity and how they impact you and me in the areas of our business interests.

Character and integrity are in everyone, and they can be described. The distinctive marks and engravings that make up one's life do show up for others to see. The nature of what is going on inside does show up on the outside. As a result, others can describe it. When asked about someone's character or integrity, we can say that they have good, sound, solid, or stellar character. Or, we might say that they have questionable, poor, shady, or evil integrity. It's not that people do not possess character or integrity. They do. We all do. And people can see it and put descriptive words to it.

Character and integrity are properly evaluated according to a standard. In order to describe and evaluate character and integrity, there must exist a standard for us to make a proper evaluation. Is one's character described as poor, questionable, or wanting? According to who or what? Is one's integrity powerful, shady, evil, or great? Again, according to who or what? Unfortunately, many use themselves as the standard by which character and integrity are evaluated. Funny how they generally find their personal character and integrity on the positive side of the equation and evaluate others according to themselves. Having the intellectual power of an MBA but the emotional stability of a fourth grader is not a combination that will lead a company to excellence.

If you are a person that takes your faith seriously, then you understand that there does exist a standard to properly evaluate inner character and integrity. It is a source that exists outside of us. It is unchanging over time and is transcendent. It's the Bible. Its words can penetrate deep enough to reveal the thoughts and intentions of the heart. It not only gives us a clear understanding of who God is but also gives us an accurate portrait of who we are.

The source of character and integrity is found in the heart. Not in our minds and thoughts. Not in our circumstances or events. The source is in our hearts. Here is how Jesus describes it:

> *For there is no good tree which produces bad fruit; nor, on the other hand, a bad tree which produces good fruit. The good man out of the good treasure of his heart brings forth what is good; and the evil man out of the evil treasure brings for what is evil; for his mouth speaks from that which fills his heart (Luke 6:43,45).*

Where does bad fruit come from? A bad tree. Where is good fruit found? A good tree. What about the fruit that we see in a man's life? You know, the character and integrity that can be clearly seen and described as good or evil? It comes from that which fills up his heart. Make no mistake, what fills up and takes residence in our hearts will become evident in what we say and how we act. We cannot hide it. Oh, we can fake it and try to dress it up to disguise it. But spoiled fruit has a look and smell that everyone can notice. Even if we choose not to look at it ourselves, it's still there for others to describe.

Character and integrity are based on behavior. It's not about talent or giftedness. Not about skills or abilities. It's all about behavior. Behavior is what we do, one action at a time. Character is the accumulation of all our behaviors over time. A behavior is a single act of an engraving tool. Put a bunch of those nicks, marks, brush strokes, and gouges together, and you have character describing who you are. Take a cross-sectional look at your life, and you will see all the qualities that make up the integrity of your heart.

There are two areas of life where our heart is consistently on display for everyone to see. One is at home and the other is at work. We can play, pretend, and put a veneer on our hearts in many areas of life, but at home, we always default back to the reality of our hearts. Our spouses and kids know us well. Really, really well. The same can be said for the workplace, especially if we are in positions of leadership and responsibility where we make daily (sometimes hourly) decisions that have consequences. What we treasure in our hearts comes out in all those decisions. Decisions for good or decisions for evil. Decisions that are good for others. Decisions that have only our best interests in mind.

That is the reality of our hearts in the workplace. It's like leading a full staff meeting with your team, only you must do so while standing in front of everyone. And all that you're wearing is one of those "one size fits all" hospital examination gowns. These are the one-size-fits-all pieces of fabric or paper for those who are five-foot-six and weigh less than 150 pounds. All of our clothes and our dignity are sitting in a bag in the corner of the examination room. For most of us, we are exposed! No matter which way we try to turn to cover up some part of our body, another part becomes visible. No matter which way we twist or turn in one of these garments of humiliation, some area that we want hidden becomes visible.

This is character and integrity of the heart on display at the workplace. Sigh . . .

Now, who's ready for some good news?

The heart can be changed. And since the heart can be changed, then our character and integrity can be changed. This is an incredible reality that people of faith can experience in their lives.

And it shows up in the workplace daily.

Listen to what the prophet Ezekiel proclaimed to those who pledged their allegiance to the One true God:

> *Moreover, I will give you a new heart and put a new spirit within you; and I will remove their heart of stone from your flesh and give you a heart of flesh. And I will put My Spirit within you and cause you to walk in My statutes, and you will be careful to observe My ordinances (Ezekiel 36:26–27).*

Did you catch that? A new heart to replace the old. His Spirit works in us and through us, and He is causing us to now live in ways that reflect and represent Him rather than a life that is continually wanting to reflect the sludge in our hearts and represent our interests above all others.

Selflessness begins to replace selfishness. Humility and courage grow to overcome pride and fear. New and life-giving desires are growing to overcome the decay that was so abundant in our hearts and lives.

And people begin to observe what is going on in our hearts as we begin to manifest a different character and a new wholeness of integrity.

Want some more good news? Your work is a center stage for this new heart to show up. Work is an incredible vehicle in which what is inside of us gets revealed so that it is observable to those outside of us. Look at how God Himself displays His attributes through His work:

> *For since the creation of the world His invisible attribute,*
> *His eternal power and divine nature, have been clearly*
> *seen, being understood through what has been made, so*
> *that they are without excuse (Romans 1:20).*

We get to understand those unseen qualities of His heart (His power and His nature) by observing that which He made. His work reveals His heart. What cannot be visibly seen can be deeply understood through the things He has made.

The same is true for us. What we make. What we produce. What service we provide. Whatever our hands find to do will become center stage for our hearts to be on display. Do you realize that one of the reasons that He gave you a new heart is for it to be put on display in the workplace? Can you grasp that He wants to put your new heart on display through the paradigm of your daily work because it reflects back to the One that gave you and me a new heart? People of faith that have been given a new heart and a new Spirit are part of His marketing plan to a world that needs to know who He is.

Do not believe for a second the lie that work is only secular and holds little if any spiritual value. The workplace is an environment that reveals the hearts of people like none other. And He wants to change your heart and then place you right in the midst of it. Jesus told of the intimate connection between our heart and our treasure. He said that where your treasure is, there your heart will be also. Want to see someone's heart? Follow the money.

Here is a simple definition of economics: it's where people and money meet, the place where hearts are revealed like no other, a display case for personal character and integrity.

God gave you a new heart and then places you in an environment where the hearts of people are being revealed daily.

He wants to show off your new heart at the intersection of people and money. Don't tell me that work is only secular and has no spiritual value! It can be a deeply sacred mission that not only reveals who you are but also Whose you are. Your work, your vocation, your calling, your sending is all working together to honor Him, benefit others, and giving you deep fulfillment and satisfaction.

That is a reality for people of faith when they connect their faith with their business interests. What they value most (their faith) connects deeply, intimately, and powerfully with the area where they spend most of their waking hours (their work).

What a way to live.

Makes you look forward to Monday.

Now, go and make an impact.

Chapter Five

SKILL AND SERVICE

And let our people also learn to engage in good deeds to meet pressing needs, that they may not be unfruitful.
Titus 3:14

In this final chapter in Section One, "Deeper Faith," I want to not only introduce a new topic, but I also want to pull all the previous concepts together and put a nice bow on everything. I really love simplicity. I appreciate it when a plan comes together. I love it when I can see how concepts interconnect and create something easily understood.

And incredibly powerful.

Work is greatly valued by God. He created it and made it deep, rich, and purposeful. However, many people of faith do not grasp the value of work, and as a result, this creates seams and gaps in their faith and in their lives. By connecting our faith with our business interests, we begin to close the gaps in our faith journey and move toward becoming seamless in our living.

To help connect our faith with our business interests, we have looked at a few biblical concepts to help us deepen our faith and bridge the spaces that trip us up. Specifically, our calling helps us draw incredibly near to God and embrace the tasks and missions He has prepared us for and sends us into. Calling profoundly affects us as individuals. It makes us into more selfless and passionate leaders.

Stewardship gives us the proper focus on growing and developing the people, opportunities, and resources we have been given responsibility for. Stewardship brings a healthy growth and culture to a business organization.

Calling gives you a vision of where you need to take your business, and what it will look like in the months and years ahead. Stewardship gives you the mission on how you are going to get there with the people, opportunities, and resources you have . . . as well as the ones you need to complete the mission.

Throughout this entire journey, character and integrity are put on display. What God is putting inside of you will leak out and impact every place you go and every task you put your hand to. Your work is a vehicle for letting the world see what is inside of you as it gets expressed.

And it's a lot more effective than the fish emblem on the back of someone's car.

One of my favorite passages of Scripture ties all these concepts together. It's found in Psalms 78:70–72.

He also chose David His servant, and took him from the sheepfolds; from the care of ewes with suckling lambs He brought him to shepherd Jacob His people, and Israel His inheritance. So, he shepherds them according to the integrity of his heart and guided them with his skillful hands.

God chose David. He called David. Just like God chose and called you.

David was called to serve. David was a king. David was a warrior. David was a musician and wrote Scripture. Yet, David was also given this mandate to serve. Your mandate as a person of faith in the marketplace is to serve.

David was to shepherd a nation. Not just manage it, but shepherd it. Care for it and make it grow. Not just part of the nation, but the people . . . and the resources and all the opportunities that came about. Stewardship! David was called to steward a nation, and you are called to steward a business, division, or corporation.

And the summary of how David did this? He did this with integrity of heart and skillful hands. What can be the dominant characteristics of how we lead our businesses? Integrity and skill.

Simple yet incredibly powerful.

So, let's dive into skills. What exactly is skill? Where does it come from? What is it for?

Once again, let's look into the origin of the word, as it will bring clarity and depth to our understanding of skill. The Hebrew word for skill is *hakam*. It is found throughout the Old Testament. However, *hakam* is also translated as the word *wisdom.* The meaning behind this is: if one has wisdom, then one also possesses skill. If one has skill, then one is looked upon as one who has wisdom.

Wisdom is more than just having knowledge or understanding. Knowledge is knowing facts. Understanding is when one can start connecting facts together into concepts. Wisdom is being able to take knowledge and understanding and then translating it into something useful and beneficial for others.

Being able to take facts and put them into concepts is critical for learning. Being able to take all the things that you know and then use that to benefit others in a specific way is critical for living.

A skillful doctor not only knows a lot of facts about the body and diseases, but they also understand how those facts all fit together. They are skillful when they can take all of that information and do something beneficial for someone to help them when they are sick or hurting, getting them to a state of health.

A skillful business owner not only knows the facts about a product or service but then creates something that is good and beneficial for others. The more beneficial the product or service is, the more it shows the degree of wisdom that the business owner has.

Wisdom is not just what we know. Wisdom is what we *show.* Wisdom is what others can see as we serve others. James says it this way in the book of the Bible by his name: "Who among you is wise and understanding? Let him show by his good behavior his deeds in the gentleness of wisdom" (3:13).

Want to know if someone is wise? Take a good look at his good deeds and behavior. Wisdom is not found in the number of degrees one has. It's really found in the degree of deeds and behavior that is good and extended toward others.

Now, don't misunderstand what I am saying here about educational degrees. Education, training, and learning are critical in our journey toward wisdom and skill. Ignorance and stupidity are not aspirational goals we should pursue. Advanced degrees like a Ph.D. or master's degrees can be really useful as well. But, if all that education and study does not translate into helping and serving others, then what good is it?

In God's economy, wisdom and skill are given so that we can serve others. Otherwise, we become puffed up, self-absorbed, and not of much use at all.

So, where does skill come from?

Ability and talent we were *given* by God.

All of us have certain natural abilities and talents. They were intentionally and specifically given to us when God created us. Take a look at Psalm 139:

> *For Thou didst form my inward parts; Thou didst weave me in my mother's womb. I will give thanks to Thee for I am fearfully and wonderfully made; wonderful are Th works, and my soul knows it very well.*

To be *wonderfully made* means to be made "with distinction." Not by chance. Not by accident. But intentional.

To be *distinct* means that you are made in such a way that makes you unique and separates you from others.

Naturally athletic with speed and strength? Designed that way.

Science and math have always been easy for you to understand? Made that way.

Able to look at problems and just know how to fix them? Yep, by design.

Have an ear for music, can play different instruments, or sing like a bird? Again, by design.

Have an entrepreneurial spirit in you that can take an idea and turn it into a product or service that others benefit from, and they just must have it? Fearfully and wonderfully made.

What are your skills, talents, and abilities? God specifically put those into your life to make you unlike anyone else. Before He put you into your mother's womb, He already had His eye and creative genius focused on you.

Development we take personal *responsibility* for.

God gave us skills. We have the responsibility to develop them and make the most of them.

How do we do that? Here are a few ways:

- Education: we learn as much as we can from others.
- Training: we continually put our wisdom and skills to the test to make them even better.
- Experience: circumstances and life lessons that help us to refine and sharpen our skills.

- Maturity: growing in getting a black belt in wisdom. You're the one who others seek out for help.
- Mindset: being a faithful steward that continually wants to grow, develop, get better, and serve others.

Taking responsibility to develop our skills is how we can become more effective in the translation of what we know and understand into something useful and beneficial for others!

The Holy Spirit *empowers* it.

Take a look at Exodus 31.

*Now the LORD spoke to Moses, saying "See, I have called by name Bezalel, the son of Uri, the son of Hur, of the tribe of Judah. **And I have filled him with the Spirit of God** in wisdom, in understanding, in knowledge, and in all kinds of craftsmanship, to make artistic designs for work in gold, in silver, and in bronze, and in the cutting of stones for settings, and in the carving of wood, that he may work in all kinds of craftsmanship. And behold, I Myself have appointed with him Oholiab, the some of Ahisamach, of the tribe of Dan; and in the hearts of all who are skillful I have put skill, that they may make all that I have commanded you . . . (emphasis mine).*

God put His Spirit into a group of blue-collar workers to work on the tabernacle. Craftsman. Artists. Designers. All working with gold, silver, wood, and stone. God *calls them by name* and *puts His Spirit into them* as well as *wisdom, understanding, knowledge, and skill* so they can do the work He set them apart to do.

Take a look at your place and responsibilities at work.

You have been called by God and He wants to fill you with His Spirit so knowledge, understanding, wisdom, and skill will show up in your life and at your work. This is one of the incredible benefits that people of faith have in the marketplace. The common grace of God has given natural talent and abilities to everyone He created. The common grace of God allows all people the opportunity to develop their skills through education, training, experience, and maturity. But only those who have placed their allegiance, trust, and faith in God can be filled with His Spirit and see it manifest in their skills at work.

Does this mean that our skills are better than anyone else's? Of course not. But can we pray specifically that God would fill and control our lives as His people and ask that He would improve our skills so we can better serve others?

Absolutely!

Let me ask you this: When was the last time you asked God to improve your skills at work? Have you ever prayed and asked God to improve your skills at work?

Let me also ask you this: Does praying for God to increase and improve your skills at work sound . . . well, you know . . . selfish? It certainly can be. If the focus is all on you. But, when you desire better skills so God is honored and others are served through your skills, then PRAY!

You were uniquely designed by God.

You were specifically trained and developed through the sovereign hand of God.

You can be powerfully filled with His Spirit.

Why? So that you can take that knowledge and understanding and translate it into something good and beneficial for others: serving!

Connecting Skills and Integrity in the Workplace

David served and led Israel with the integrity of his heart and guided the people with his skillful hands. Skills and integrity are individually good, but it's best when they show up together.

There are those in the workplace that have high integrity but low skills. That's *potential* that can get better over time. Skills can certainly be taught and improved over time.

There are those that have great skills but low integrity. That's a *problem* that will only get worse over time.

Then there are those that possess great skills and integrity. That's when potential has now become *potent and powerful.*

Let me ask a few questions about skill and integrity:

- Do you know anyone who you would describe as having potential?
- Have you encountered anyone that has skill but poor integrity? You know, a problem.
- Know anyone that when you think about their lives in the marketplace, you might say, "That's powerful!"

Now, how would your team, employees, customers, and vendors describe *you*? Be honest with yourself. Write down about ten words that would best describe you at work. This is your current reality of having what is inside of you manifesting on the outside for others to see.

Now, how would you like to be described?

You don't have to stay at the place where you are at. In fact, God has His own mission statement He is going to work in the lives of those who put their faith in Him to change their hearts. He loves you where He found you, and He loves you enough not to let you stay there. He wants to put His Spirit into you and then show off what He can do through you.

Friends, allow God to work in your lives. Take seriously your personal responsibility to develop your skills. Take seriously having God change your heart and fill you with His Spirit. Let God transform you and then place you into the workplace to transform it.

You can be on your way to *potent and powerful.*

Integrity of heart and skill of hands. With them, you can lead a nation as David did. And you can run a corporation or department or business. It can show up in the largest or smallest of jobs.

Let it show up in you and in the place where you work. As the great reformer, Martin Luther, has said,

"The way that a cobbler loves his neighbor as himself is by making a good pair of shoes."

We live in a world that is sinful and broken. Problems are everywhere.

God can redeem a man's heart and soul. He can also redeem his mind and hands. Could it be that He redeemed you to be part of the solution to some of the world's problems? You better believe it!

Now, let's get to work!

SECTION TWO
BUILDING A BETTER BUSINESS

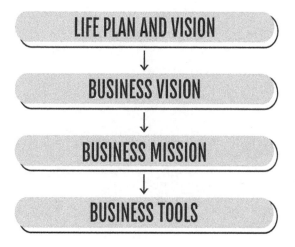

LIFE PLAN AND VISION

↓

BUSINESS VISION

↓

BUSINESS MISSION

↓

BUSINESS TOOLS

Chapter Six

MAKING A LIFE PLAN
WITH A PRIORITY OF ONE

*As for the days of our life, they contain seventy years, or if
due to strength, eighty years. So, teach us to number our
days, that we may present to Thee a heart of wisdom.*
Psalm 90:10 and 12

*When the risen Christ is central, you know what is
peripheral. Never confuse the two.*
Stuart Briscoe

I'm pretty certain that some of you reading this chapter are
wondering why we are starting off by talking about a life
plan? After all, isn't this the section on building a business and

developing a business plan? Yes, it is, but the truth is that an effective and healthy business plan comes out of an effective and healthy life plan. A life plan and a business plan should not compete with each other over the limited energy, time, and resources that you have. They should enhance each other, leading to greater clarity, success, satisfaction, fulfillment, and decision making. It should bring about less stress, conflicts, frustration, and regret.

Let me ask you this: How much time and effort have you put into planning a vacation? How about a major purchase, like a car or a new home? What about your daughter's wedding?

At work, how much time is spent planning today, next week, the following quarter, or the fiscal year? We are great at planning so many things!

But what about a life?

Let me give you an example. A few years ago, I heard a retired CEO talking about his experience mentoring a young business owner. The young man was happily married, had two little darling daughters, and a growing business doing $10M a year. His business peers and others in the industry kept telling him that his booming business could easily pass $100M soon. So, the young man asked the older CEO how he grows his business to $100M.

"You're asking the wrong question," replied the wise veteran. "In our times together, you said that you want your marriage to grow strong and that you put a high value on being a dad to your little girls. So, let's look at the time that you think you should invest in these areas that you believe are important to you."

After working through a weekly schedule, they concluded that the young man had forty-five to fifty hours left that he could put toward his business.

"So the question you should be asking is not how big I can grow this company, but rather, how effectively can I grow this business on forty-five to fifty hours a week," said the old CEO.

That is called *perspective*. A wise and powerful perspective. It shows how an effective business plan must come out of an effective life plan. This way, the business does not become the master of one's life and begins to compete with and devour other important aspects of life. Business can offer so many wonderful opportunities for us and others to enjoy. But, when it takes the place of master in our lives, it will demand that we sacrifice everything else for its cause.

A well-thought-out life plan allows you to watch, evaluate, and care for all the areas of life that you are responsible for . . . and cause them to grow into a synergistic and fruitful life rather than one that is unfocused, chaotic, and yields regret.

So how do we create a great life plan that will get you where you really want to go? There are some very common strategies used to develop a life plan. Many of them ask that you pick a variety of categories in life you think are important to you. You rate them according to how you think they currently are. Next, you determine how you would like those individual areas to look like in the next three years, ten years, or at the end of your life. Then, you begin to map out how to get from your current reality to your preferred future. One helpful tool people use to bring some clarity to this task is to have you imagine what your funeral would look like. Who would be there, and what would you like to have them say about you? What would you like to have written on your gravestone?

This imaginative tool is quite good, and it does help to dig beneath the surface of life to help us understand what things are really important over those that are not. But this tool just doesn't dig deep enough to really focus our thinking.

For people of faith to think about what a loving spouse, children, and close friends would have to say is important. But what will God have to say at that time is vital. Upon being ushered into His presence at the moment of your last breath, will you hear Him speak the words, "Well done good and faithful servant?"

Now work backward from that. You hope your spouse and children share thoughts full of love, respect, and loyalty. You hope your friends will talk of your character, love, and impact. There will be those who will weep because you are now gone. The people that have been impacted will say so. The fruit of a life that was passionately lived well will be the focus.

This is a perspective that looks deep into life and encourages you to make decisions and choices that get you there. Decisions and choices that are not to be made someday but are being made right now.

This is what beginning with the end in mind should really look like.

We know how we want this part of life to end, but how do we get there? For many of us, when we want to get our life in order, we seek to "get our priorities in order." So we start to create lists of what should be first, second, third, or fifteenth. So what is on your list? Go ahead, write them down. I'll wait . . .

Let's imagine that we are on a Zoom call with all of the other people that just made their lists. Let's have everyone share their list of priorities. We hear from Sam, Zach, Caleb, and some guy that goes by Bubba. We hear from Bethany, Amy, Alissa, Emma, and Grace. And you.

Let me ask some questions:

- Whose got the best list?
- If your list is not the same as another's list, then who has the wrong priorities?
- What if your list changes next year? Were you wrong in your priorities this year . . . or next year?
- If you believe that creating a list is very personal, an individual task, and we should not be concerned about how these priorities compare to others—or even to other years in our lives—then do these priorities have any actual value or substance?
- If it's true that priorities are based on individual preferences that have no substantial value compared to others or even over time, then what good are they? If they have no more value than a fleeting opinion of the day, then how can we think that they are solid enough to really direct our lives?

Is there a better way to look at life? I believe so. Rather than making a list, let's make a model.

The Pentathlon of Life

There are five dominant areas of life, or institutions, that God created, and He gives us instructions in the Scriptures on how we are to live in them.

- **Individual:** He intentionally made you, and there are passages that specifically speak to our taking responsibility for our conscience, growth, behavior, and actions.
- **Family:** He created the institution of marriage and the growth of the family with children.
- **Work:** He created work as a divine institution and mandate, and there are numerous passages that speak to the behaviors and responsibilities that we are to have as we engage this institution.
- **Church:** The Body of Christ is the universal collective of His people that have been called to Him, and by responding in faith, they live for Him. This universal Body has numerous local expressions, and there are passages that speak to how the Church is to function and live out its mission here on Earth.
- **Community and Government:** Humanity gathers and lives in various sized communities, which have governing bodies that oversee and serve them. Although we see so many broken and evil expressions of these, we must understand that God has a design and intention for these institutions, and He speaks to the proper functioning of them . . . as well as our proper living within them.

Five areas of life that we find ourselves in. Five areas of life that God speaks about to us as He outlines how we should live in them. So how should we look at these to understand them better?

Life is an event. The apostle Paul uses the analogy of a race to describe life in 1 Corinthians 9 where he says, "Do you not know that those who run in a race all run, but only one receives the prize? Run in such a way that you may win."

Life. An event. A race. Five major categories.

A modern pentathlon.

The modern pentathlon has five events in which the athletes compete: running, swimming, fencing, pistol shooting, and equestrian.

Life runs a similar race: individual, family, work, church, and community. So why not create a model instead of a list, one that looks like this:

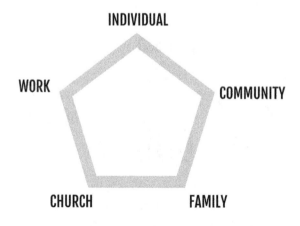

Now, I can already hear the questions coming up:

Q: Greg, I don't like your list. There are important people and activities that I have on my list, but they are not on yours. What about things like hobbies, health and fitness, or weight loss?

A: These all fall into the Individual category. These are all items you are choosing to take the time to involve yourself in.

Q: I want to prioritize a date night with my spouse and make sure I get to my kids' activities and events.

A: Family category.

Q: What about evangelism and discipleship? What about worship? For crying out loud, WHAT ABOUT GOD! At least I have God on my list, and He's on the top of it! WHERE IS GOD IN ALL OF THIS?

A: He's right where He belongs, smack dab in the center of it all.

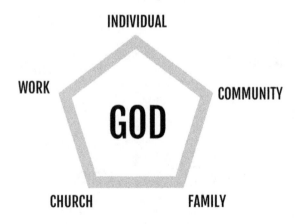

God is central to all and not just first among many. Too often, when we as Christians make a list of priorities and say that God is first, we view life as segmented areas that have very little interaction with each other. They are their own individual categories. As a result, we unknowingly put God in a box. We go to church on Sundays. And we think that is our God time. We have morning devotions. That is our God time. But too often, God is not a factor during the rest of the day or the rest of the week. He's left in the box of Sunday or during a small portion of the day. As a result, we don't meet with Him at work. Or in the community. Or in parts of our family.

Mark 12 tells of a time when a scribe came to ask Jesus a question. "What commandment is the foremost of all?"

Jesus answered, "The foremost is, Hear, O Israel! The Lord our God is One Lord; and you shall love the Lord your God with all your heart, and with all your soul, and with all your mind, and with all your strength. The second is this. You shall love your neighbor as yourself. There is no other commandment greater than these" (verses 29–31).

The scribe wants to know out of all of the commandments, what is foremost. The word *foremost* is from the Greek word *protos*. *Protos* means "first in time or place in any succession of things or persons; first in rank; first among all others." If something is *protos*, it means that it is first among all the other things that want to be first. In other words, in all of our priorities, there stands something (or Someone) above all and through all of them. Jesus declared that out of all the commandments, there stands one that is *protos* . . . foremost, first above all others, and that is to love God with everything that we are (heart, soul, mind, strength . . . being intellectual, physical, emotional, willful in our love), and then, it pours out of us to those who are around us.

Where does evangelism take place? It takes place in the home. It takes place with people at work, in the community, and in church. It takes place through individuals to other individuals.

What about discipleship? Where do we see this taking place? Again, in the home, in the church, in the community, and in the workplace.

What about worship? Again, worship is something done by individuals either alone or in a group, and it takes place in home, churches, and yes, in the workplace.

When most people are asked about their priorities, they will say they have a bunch of them. Ask them what is important in their lives, and they will say that everything seems to be important.

The Scriptures tell us that we really only have *one* priority, and that priority is Him. And that one priority gives meaning, value, dignity, and importance to all the other responsibilities that He has given us to steward.

So we are to live in the Pentathlon of Life with a Priority of One.

Take a look at the people around you. All of them are living in some, or all, of these five areas, and there is a default setting in their lives impacting all of these areas. We all have a default setting! It's what sits and lives in the center of our life model and is the primary impact and driving force affecting all the areas of our lives.

Unfortunately, what is most common in the Pentathlon of Life is the Priority of *me*. And this trinity of Me, Myself, and I show up at work, home, church, and in the community. It is evident wherever they choose to go and whatever they choose to do. Oh sure, they can fake it at times. Wear some camouflage. Pretend, act the part, play the game. But what is inside always comes out. It's a default setting. We all have one. The question is, "What's yours?"

If you're not sure, just ask around to those in these five areas. They should be able to tell you. After all, they have seen and experienced it for some time now.

So we have five jurisdictions we find ourselves in and a single priority impacting them all. These are wrapped up in a working model that is like an athletic pentathlon because there are some striking similarities between an athletic pentathlon and this race called life. Let's look at them.

- The pentathlon is a diversity of events that would determine the *overall quality* of an athlete over a broad range of skills. Originally, the pentathlon had five events that would be necessary for a soldier that found himself behind enemy lines. It was used to determine who would be an ideal soldier. Later, it became the modern pentathlon with athletic events to determine who is the best athlete. Similarly, the pentathlon of life reveals the *kind of person or the quality of a person* over a broad range of responsibilities. Want to know what kind of person someone is? Look at these areas in the pentathlon of life, and you will get a good picture of the quality of their lives. The pentathlon of life is really quite revealing.

- In the athletic pentathlon, great success in one area does not guarantee success in another. Just because you are really good at running, does not mean that you can ride a horse. You might be good with the sword, but can only dog paddle in the pool? It's true in athletics. It's also true in life. Just because you are great at home with the spouse and kids, it does not guarantee that you can do well at work, church, or community. You might be an effective CEO, but that is not a guarantee that you're skills or attitudes will spill over into your marriage or community. The pentathlon of life sure has a way of revealing our strengths . . . and exposing our weaknesses.

- Hard work and training are essential for success. In athletics, it is difficult (even rare) to attain success through natural talent and ability alone. Constant training and hard work are essential. The same is true in these critical areas of life we have been looking at. Continuing with the analogy of life being a race, the apostle Paul continues on in 1 Corinthians 9 by writing, "And everyone who competes in the games exercises *self-control in all things.* They do it to receive a perishable wreath, but we an imperishable. Therefore, I run in such a way, as *not without aim;* I box in such a way, as not beating the air; but I *buffet my body* and make it my slave, lest possibly, after I have preached to others, I myself should be disqualified" (verses 24–

27). Here he states that we should have self-control in all things. That's *discipline*. We are to have aim and certainty. That's *wisdom*. And we are to buffet our bodies and make them our slaves. That's *sacrifice*. Discipline, wisdom, and sacrifice are necessary for athletic success. It's vital for success in life as well. In fact, anything of excellence requires these qualities! Parenting and marriage are not easy, and if you want to be excellent at them, it requires discipline, wisdom, and sacrifice. The same is true for work. Or church. Or being a person of excellence in your community.

• In the pentathlon, there are many events but only one prize or reward. Awards were not given out for individual events but a composite score for all the events was given, and a single award was given to the person with the highest overall score. So what about people of faith and the lives they are living? How does this work? 1 Corinthians 9:25 tells us that we run this race called "life" because we will receive as a reward a wreath (singular). In 1 Corinthian 3:10–15, it tells us that our life's works and deeds will be revealed with fire to show their quality. The result of what remains is given to us as a reward (again singular). The Scriptures tell us that this wreath or reward will be manifested as a crown. Each of us will have a unique crown that somehow will picture the life that we lived, probably with embedded jewels and precious stones representing the good deeds that honored God and benefited others. It will be a reward for the pentathlon of life that we lived. Five very significant areas of life. One reward symbolizing a composite score of all of life put together. Everything is factored in. Everything is important. Everything has value. Now, here's the best part: What do we do with these jeweled covered crowns? Wear them for eternity as a billboard for how totally awesome we are? Nope. Revelation 4:10 tells us that we will cast our crowns before the throne of God as an expression of incredible worship. Let that sink in for just a moment. What kind of crown do you want to have to offer during this incredible expression of worship? Don't bring one of those Burger King kind. Bring your absolute best and let your joy run deep!

- In an athletic pentathlon, you receive a score in every event based upon your performance. The better you perform, the higher your score. However, even if you perform poorly in an event, you are still awarded points. You could be terrible at one of the events, and you will still be given some points. Not exactly like today's participation trophies, but you get the idea. The only way that you receive zero points in an event is by being disqualified. That means cutting corners and breaking the rules. And the way that the athletic pentathlon is set up, if you receive zero points in any one event, there is no possibility of winning, no matter how well you do in the other events. Life can be very similar. There is an issue of disqualification that we, as people of faith, need to be aware of. The apostle Paul said that he competed in life with discipline and sacrifice so that after he had preached to others, "I myself will not be disqualified" (1 Corinthians 9:27). This issue of disqualification is not saying the secure and eternal salvation that is given to all who believe in Christ can be lost. What it is implying is that failure in any of these areas is devastating to a life. What good is it if a person is great at the workplace but a total failure at home because he continually breaks the principles of being a godly husband and father? What do we call a church leader that grows a megachurch but is caught with his pants off with another woman? A failure. Or the devoted church member who is at every service, Bible study, and short-term mission trip, but at work, he is a pain in the blessed assurance because he is lazy; his work is done poorly; he shows up late and leaves early, and he has the work ethic of a third grader? Failure! Now, I don't want you to take this aspect of the pentathlon too far. Do we all fail at times? Yes. Do we struggle in certain areas of life? Absolutely. Are there things that we have done that are characterized as cutting corners, breaking rules, or worse? Yep. But let me remind you that this is where repentance comes in. This is where grace and mercy triumph over judgment. However, the point of this is that consistent disobedience and rebellion in any area of life will have consequences. And it's not pretty.

- The events of the pentathlon are the same for every contestant, but the race is not exactly the same for every person. Every participant is unique. Each participant has a unique set of skills, talents, and abilities. This means their training and focus on the events will be unique. But the goal is the same for every contestant. *Run the race in such a way that you may win!* So, where are you right now? Older or younger? Run in such a way that you may win! Do you own a small business with a few employees, or are you sitting in the C suite with 5000 employees? Run in such a way that you may win. Got two little kids at home and going through diapers by the hundreds and sleep is measured in minutes, or do you have a house full of teenagers or kids off at college? Whatever circumstances you are in will dictate how you will train for these events. But in all these things *run*!

Throughout your life, you are given a number of responsibilities that include some significant people, some time and resources, and a million decisions that have to be made. And through all of this, there is a single dominant priority that leads and empowers you all the way.

What a way to live.

It's time to run!

Chapter Seven

BUSINESS VISION AND WHAT COULD BE

Vision often begins with the inability to accept things the way they are. There is always a moral element to vision. Vision carries with it a sense of conviction. Anyone with a vision will tell you this is not merely something that could be done. This is something that should be done. This is something that must happen.

Andy Stanley

A great deal has been written about having a vision for your business. A proper vision is a catalyst for growth, productivity, health, and fulfillment in your business.

Notice I said a *proper vision.*

Before we launch into this topic, I want to be clear on some things. Not everything that is written or talked about concerning vision is good. In fact, some of it is crap because it's based upon lies. Here is a sample of what I am talking about:

- "God will bless all of your dreams if you only have enough faith!"
- "If you can see it, and believe it, then you can achieve it!"
- "The answers are all in you. Success is already in your heart and all you need to do is let it out!"
- "What the mind can conceive the body (and the business) can achieve!"
- "With a proper vision you can do anything that you want. You are the only limitation to being unlimited!"
- "Just follow your heart. God, please bless all the desires of my heart."

Well, what if your heart is full of pride and selfishness? What if your dreams honestly just suck?

When I hear or read this kind of nonsense, I want to throw a flag on the field and call "BS." Strong language? Nope. I can be stronger. Too many people have fallen for this thinking and have found themselves discouraged, defeated, and disillusioned because the trail of fairy dust met up with reality and got blown away.

Now the flip side of "I can do anything I envision" is the passive belief that "I can't do anything." As a result, we choose to just stay in the narrow lane of other's expectations of us and our business, believing mediocracy is a great, safe place in which to travel. This, too, is wrong. It's lazy, passive, and foolish. As people of faith, we need to understand there is a real spiritual enemy that loves to tell us to "sit down, shut up, and just stay where you are! Don't move!"

Can I address another common problem with Christians in business? Many are afraid of growth and success. They see it as worldly, selfish, and prideful. That can certainly be true. But growth can also be embedded in humility, passion, generosity, and faithful stewardship.

A few years ago, I went with a team of physicians to Moldova to visit a Christian hospital in the capital city. Our mission was to train and encourage the local physicians on new surgical and medical advancements. The hospital had a small dental clinic with two dentists, and they had never had a dentist come to help them. Enter Dr. Greg. After observing the two dentists, the staff, facility, and procedures, they asked what I thought. So I told them what I heard and saw over the past three days:

- Two dentists working out of one treatment chair each. Each dentist with the support of only one assistant.
- An assisting staff with very limited training and skills, whose only job is to vacuum spit and clean up after the doctors.
- A multitude of patients waiting weeks, or sometimes months, to get in because this clinic offered the best dental care in the city. These were people that paid cash for their dental service.

- A large unused waiting room next to their clinic with no future plans for its use.

Then I gave them the recommendations I envisioned for their clinic:

- Expand the current clinic into the unused waiting room and put in more treatment rooms.
- Hire two more doctors and some support staff
- Train the assisting team to actually assist with procedures so that better care is delivered more efficiently.
- Have the two current dentists come back and shadow at our clinic for a week at my expense and see how new policies, procedures, and systems can greatly impact their care and productivity. Show them how they can work effectively and efficiently with each doctor having two or three treatment chairs each.

I then told them I can easily see this clinic increasing their productivity and profitability by 400–500 percent (I kept my estimates on the low side so as to not overwhelm them or have them laugh in my face).

Now, seeing that these dentists were younger believers in the faith, and they had grown up in a Communist country until recently, their response was what I thought it would be.

"That sounds selfish to have that kind of wealth."

That's when I dropped a truth bomb on them.

"Who said that any of this was for you!" I paused to let the owner recover from the initial shock that covered his face.

"I'm thinking that this clinic can expand to the point of being the major contributor in financing this hospital. I can see this clinic becoming a shining city on a hill and an incredible blessing to this community and all who work here. Dentists will want to train then be employed here. Jobs will be created, which will increase the standard of living for the community. The people with pain, misery, infection, and disease, which is so common in the city, will now have a place to find quick and effective care. And I see *you* leading it."

I absolutely love the look on a face when the lightbulb turns on.

As you develop your business vision, remember this. *It's not all about you.* If you reach the end of your vision, and the only one who has benefited from the journey is you, then you have failed.

This is why we began with a theological, faith-based reality to build our business vision upon. Developing your business vision is united in what God is *calling* you to do. His vision for your business is becoming your vision for your business. You can't do everything, but you were certainly made for something. It's how you were made—intentionally, strategically, and with distinction. Why? For a purpose! You were made for this!

The Value of a Business Vision

Here are a few reasons why a clear vision for your business is so valuable:

- It provides a clear direction where your business needs to go. It provides clarity, one of the most important growth factors for any business, organization, group, or family.

- Knowing where you want to go decreases the chance you wind up somewhere else less desirable.
- Knowing where you want to go will allow you to get there faster without taking wasteful and unnecessary detours along the way.
- Knowing where you want to go and what you want the business to look like allows you to evaluate your progress along the way.
- Knowing where you want to go allows you to understand when your trajectory is starting to move off course. Course corrections come sooner, are easier to implement, and the potential loss of time and resources is diminished.
- A clear and compelling vision gets your team rowing together in the same direction. This is powerful.
- A clear and compelling vision draws other like-minded people to your business who want to work with you.
- A clear vision helps to hire better people and pass on those who don't fit your organization. This greatly decreases the amount of Advil you take because of problem employees.
- A clear and compelling vision creates a healthy culture in your business that attracts more customers, enjoys more satisfied employees, experiences less employee turnover, has less wasteful expenses, and sees greater productivity.

Now, who doesn't want a piece of that action!

So, let's get started! There are some tools that you will use to help you think about your business vision, clarify your existing vision, or bring a deeper conviction and resolve concerning the vision for your business. You will be able to download the tools at thekalosbusinessgroup.com/tools.

Here is what I will not do. I will not tell you what your business vision should be. This is *your* vision, and it is deeply connected to what God is calling you to do and who to become. This is more of you and God, not you and me. Believe me, you want Him as the originator of the vision, not me. He created universes. I get a list of four things from my wife to pick up at the store, and I usually come home with three. What I will do is ask questions. Lots of questions. Hopefully, deep-thinking questions that will allow you the opportunity to get really clear on your business vision.

Questions For Clarifying Vision for Owners

1. **Whose am I?** We are working on the vital area of your work. It's one of the important parts of the Pentathlon of Life and in the middle of it all, something is central. Remember? It's having a Priority of One. So before you move on, have you determined what (or Who) is your Priority of One? If you are a person of faith, really trying to connect your faith with your business, then this is the critical first step. Whose are you? Maybe now is a good time to put the book down and have a heart-to-heart with God. Are you seeking a calling and a vision?

Ask Him. Seek Him. Do you feel like a hypocrite saying that God is central when you know in your heart that He is not? Who of us has not been there at one time or another? But don't stay there! Repent, confess, and ask for forgiveness and a renewed heart and faith. He tells us that He is faithful and just to forgive us and to cleanse us of our unrighteousness. Dedicate this time to Him and ask Him to clearly speak to you and give you the direction needed to steward this business He has placed in your hands.

2. **Who am I?** How have you been fearfully and wonderfully made? What are your strengths and weaknesses? List your talents, gifts, and skills. How will they come into play in carrying out the vision?

3. **How have I been prepared for such a time as this?** What training, experience, or education has played a role in bringing you where you are at this time? How does it shape your vision? What are the past events that have significantly shaped you? Lessons from a time of trial? Times when you have experienced great victory or success? How have these experiences worked together to prepare you to take on your vision?

4. **What do I desire to do?** I believe that things, desire, and passion are critical for vision. If you are going to follow a vision, a preferred future destination, then you will run into obstacles, roadblocks, and setbacks. Count on it. And to get through them, or around them, you will need a good portion of passion and desire to support your heart and soul through the difficult

times. I believe that topics of passion and desire have not been addressed correctly and have been thought of as something negative. Sure, there are negative expressions of this seen as worldly passions and selfish desires. Those are abundant. But salvation and new life that is ushered in by God brings us a new heart. We are to transform our minds (Romans 12:2). God does not want to take away our passions and desires; He wants to redeem them. Worldly desires become righteous desires. Selfish ambition changes into godly ambitions. Delight yourself in God, and He will give you the desires of your heart (Psalms 37:4). Seek Him and His desires for what He calls you to, then they will become the desires in your heart to passionately live out. So what are those thoughts that keep you up at night? What are those dreams you keep thinking about when you are all alone? What "could be" makes the adrenaline rush a little more in your body?

5. **Why do I desire this?** Who benefits from this vision? Here are three categories to write about:
   - How does the pursuit of this vision honor God?
   - How does the pursuit of this vision benefit others? Who? How are they benefited?
   - How does the pursuit of this vision satisfy me, fulfill me, and bring me joy?

Those times when that recurring thought keeps rolling around in your head (when you are alone, as you are trying to go to sleep, as you are thinking about the future of your business, etc.), if you see it is indeed honoring, good, and beneficial, then it could be that God is speaking to your heart. Ask Him to clarify it. Ask Him if these thoughts are really from Him. This will be a deep season of prayer and drawing near to Him. It will deepen your faith. You could be at the starting blocks of a great adventure. If you honestly evaluate these desires and only see a benefit for you or see that these desires are infected with some aspect of sin, then the origin of these desires are either from the mind, set upon fleshly desires, or from a dark spiritual enemy. If this is the case, then treat it accordingly. Treat it like the rabid wolf it is. Don't keep it in your home, thinking you can tame it and live in peace with it. Speak truth to the lies. And drag that wolf out in the street and shoot it.

6. **What does the preferred vision look like?** What does the outcome look like in the next year, three years from now, or at the end of your days? Pick a timeframe to work on. It will not be the same for everyone. If you are in your late twenties, have a wife and baby at home, and are in the early days of starting your business, then your vision may be just to get through today and hope to have some cash at the end of the month. For you, a three-month vision or just one vision would work. If you are an older executive or business owner, your vision may be looking to what this business could look like when it's time to hand the baton off to another leader. So what does that preferred future vision actually look like? Describe it in as many emotional details as

possible. What will clients see and experience? What will the business culture feel like, sound like, and look like? What will the look on employees' faces be? What will the experience be from working there? Think of Dorothy opening up the door of her house when she landed in Oz. Remember it? The picture turned from black and white to vivid color. As you tell people where it is you are taking them, let them emotionally engage with it. You are not showing them a project on an Excel spreadsheet; you are communicating a destination you are taking them to. It is solid, realistic, and compelling. Let me give you an example. When we moved into our current clinic after the flood, I really thought that would be it. No more expansion or growth. Then God began to change my heart, and a new vision began to form. I wrote down what our next expansion would be. How many other doctors and staff would we hire? How many receptionists would be needed? What new positions would be created? What would the schedules look like? . . . What the patient experience would look, feel, sound, and smell like. And what kind of clinic we could become and how our community would be benefited. Give your business, employees, and customers the benefit of experiencing something that God is calling you to do.

7. **What will this cost me?** It's getting real now. What will it cost you in time, resources, and energy to accomplish this? What will you need to give up taking this on?

8. **Am I willing to pay the price?** Leaders take the risks. Strategic risks but still risks. The leaders and owners are the ones who sign at the bottom of the papers and take responsibility. If this goes south and fails, you pay. If it goes well, then you, along with countless others, benefit. If the price of your vision is too high for you, then reevaluate your vision. That's OK. You're not the only one to be in that situation. What you can't do is quit and throw in the towel. That's not good stewardship, and too many people are needing your gifts, talents, skills, experience, and calling. They need your vision to come about.

9. **What are the obstacles that stand in the way?** There will always be something(s) that will get in the way to slow down or even stop your journey. Be honest with yourself. What are they?

10. **Who will you go to for help?** Got a dream? You'll need some advisors. Got a really big dream? Probably even more advisors and resources.

11. **When will you start?** A dream is something that continually rolls around in our heads and stays there. It becomes a vision when we take action. This is when good intentions become definite commitments. Dreams are OK. But they only stay in our heads. Vision is what impacts others and becomes a force for good. Your vision for your business can't just stay in your head. There are too many people that need what God wants to do in you and through you. It's time to begin.

You have access to a list of downloadable tools and worksheets to help you gain clarity as you build and engineer the vision for your business. Go to:

www.thekalosbusinessgroup.com/tools

The Nature of Your Business and Why Does It Exist

Knowing why your business exists will certainly bring significant clarity as to where you want to take it. Here are some questions to help you answer this:

- Who is our customer or clients?
- What do they want, or what do they value?
- How do we currently serve them?
- What results am I having?
- What is something exceptional our customers or clients are looking for?
- How are we meeting their desires?
- How do we define success? What is a home run in our business?
- If I was to sell my business to another entity, and my presence, leadership, and influence were no longer there, what would change? What would be missing? What would be lacking? What would the customers or clients notice the most? How would they be impacted?
- Describe your business by using the following template:
- "This business provides (blank) to (blank) so they can have or experience (blank)."

- Now that you have described the purpose of your business in a single sentence, use one word that describes its purpose:

Is it hard to describe the purpose of your business in a single word? Absolutely. Anyone can describe the nature and purpose of their business in a paragraph. When someone really has a good grasp and understanding of their business, they can say it in a sentence. Exceptional ones can say it in a word. They really *know* their business. When necessary, they can also use a single sentence. If they need to, they can talk about their business in paragraphs. Or entire pages. But, as you listen to them expound on their business, you realize they are all manifestations, expressions, or applications of that one, single word or sentence.

Convictions

This tool will help guide you along the journey. If the vision is the path you are on, core convictions are the guardrails that help keep you on the path. These are the characteristics and distinctive qualities that describe and drive the business. These are words or phrases that say, "This is who we are, and this is how we are going to go about our business." Usually, three to six is a good number to have. Less than three might not be enough, and more than six starts to become too complex. Simple is easy to know, easy to understand, and easy to do.

Some questions to help you out:

1. What are three to six words that serve as the pillars for the actions and decision-making in your life?
2. What are some qualities or characteristics in your business that you greatly admire or ones you really want to have in your business?
3. If you were to take on a new job in a completely different industry, would these core convictions move with you? Would those that directed you now be the same that direct your new business?
4. Are these convictions able to be performed by everyone in the business?
5. For example, you really value respecting others. It's a big part of who you are, and you really want it to be part of the DNA of your business. You have a retail store that has salespeople taking care of customers, as well as a customer service department that also takes care of customers. You have a core conviction that says this:

> **Respect:** *we will treat every individual with a high level of respect and dignity, not only those we serve, but also those with whom we work.*

Can everyone do this? They should. If they can't, then they should seek employment with another organization that aligns with their personal philosophies. Respect is a choice. So is being disrespectful and dishonoring to others. This conviction gives direction and expectation to the business in each and every department. When a situation arises and they are not sure quite what to do, they do know that in all things, they will be respectful. Also, should this owner move from a retail and sales business to a service or educational situation, the pillar of respect can work there as well.

Here is what we have at both of our dental clinics, as well as at The Kalos Group:

Commitment: we will each commit to the mission of the clinic and our individual roles in fulfilling it.

Service: we strive to fulfill the needs and expectations of those we care for with the best of our abilities.

Integrity: we strive to consistently grow and develop throughout every area of the organization so that we can bring our very best in the service of others.

Skill: we bring a high level of competence and wisdom to the needs of our patients.

Passion: we bring encouragement and enthusiasm to the tasks at hand . . . and let good things run wild!

Honor: we strive to honor God in all that we do and give the proper respect to the people on our team, as well as those we serve.

Do these look familiar? It's what the first part of the book was about. These convictions are as serious as a heart attack to me. It hasn't always been that way, but over a number of years, this is what has captured my heart, soul, and mind. As a result, this is how I want to characterize my dental clinic. And a pediatric clinic. And a speaking and coaching business. And what I thought I should write about.

So, get your convictions out of your head and down on a piece of paper. There will be times as you travel on the path of your vision when the view will get foggy, and you won't be able to see very far ahead. You won't be able to see what might be coming around the bend in the next quarter, the next month, or even next Tuesday. That's why you need some solid guardrails on the side. That's why they are there. To guide you all along the way.

A clear and compelling vision is vital for your business. Your employees will greatly benefit from this kind of clear direction to a preferred future. Most of them are probably longing for it. There are clients and customers that are drawn to businesses where they experience the culture that is formed by these values. They become loyal customers. They become vocal spokespeople in the community (and on the Internet), drawing even more people that want to experience the culture of your business, one shaped by your convictions and driven by a clear and passionate vision.

There are people who need what you have to offer and what your business "could be."

Chapter Eight

YOUR BUSINESS MISSION:
Stewardship
(How to get from where you are to where you need to go)

I f vision announces where you are headed, then mission describes how you are going to get there. Vision answers the questions of *where* and *why* while mission answers the *what* and *how*. Now that you have the vision and know what direction you need to move, you're going to need the stuff to get you there. The bigger your vision, the more stuff you will probably need. You're going to need people, resources, and the right opportunities. This is the practical theology of stewardship.

Every business has these three components: people, resources, and opportunities. These are the building blocks that make a business grow. But as we all know, not all businesses grow. Most fail within the first five years of their starting date.

There are those that do experience a steady and consistent growth that produces some great results. These are the ones that make the most out of the people, resources, and opportunities they have.

Now, before we dive into mission, I want to clarify some expectations or assumptions. If you think I am going to be telling you how to run your business . . . nope. People picking up this book may be in the food, healthcare, real estate, manufacturing, construction, or IT business. Plus, many more. I cannot begin to know the inner workings of these industries. But you do. You know your industry so much better than I do. What I will share with you are some insights that will allow you to evaluate those specific components of your business and make them even better.

Let's dive in.

People

We will begin with the most important resource in your business, and that is *people*. Let me explain: People are more important than systems, policies, or procedures. Why? Because it is your people who are running your systems, embracing your policies, and carrying out your procedures. You might have the greatest systems in your industry, but if you have donkeys running them, it's not going to go well. Switch this around. If you have some mediocre systems but some great people working them, then you are going to do alright. The same is true with policies and procedures. You can have the thickest policy manual written by a team of business attorneys, but if all you have are poor employees, then all that manual does is tell you how much your team really sucks. Take some great people and put them on a team with half a piece of paper that says, "Let's show them what we can do today!" and watch them do something special.

When I talk to dentists about the importance of people, this is how I present it. See if you see some similarities in your particular industry. I start by asking what differentiates one dental office from another. Specifically, *your* dental office from the others in your community. For the most part, dentists have access to many of the same resources: all have received excellent training and have skills; all have access to buy the latest and greatest equipment; there are no supplies or products they cannot get; banks are generally willing to give out loans to build facilities, equipment, or expand; they have equal access to additional training, education, or consultants that would love to take their money. Since we all have equal access to all of these resources, then what can possibly differentiate one office from another? That's right, it's the people. They provide the services. They run the systems. They answer the phones. They have face-to-face conversations with clients, patients, or customers. They are a significant part of your business's culture. And it is one of the primary reasons that people want to do business with you. Or why they choose to go somewhere else.

I am not telling you that systems, policies, etc. are not important. They are. I am not saying that you should embrace your people and not care about the systems. This is not "either/or" but rather "both/and."

Why not have the best of *both*!

Great people with outstanding systems and resources. Now, you're looking at something that will certainly differentiate you from the rest of those in your industry. You have moved up to first string, and your team is a force to be reckoned with.

For most businesses, the greatest expense is payroll expenditures. It's the wages, benefits, paid vacation, and holiday . . . and all sorts of other things. It's a huge expense.

"But Greg, this should not be seen as an expense. It's an *investment!*"

People are only an investment when you treat them like an investment. If you hire them and spend very little focused attention on getting them to grow, then all you have is an expense. If you take the initial action of planting seeds in the ground but spend precious little time tending to them, you can call it a garden all you want. In reality, all you have is very little crop and a whole lot of weeds.

That is not an investment. That's a pain in the rear end.

Developing People

A common frustration that I hear from many business owners is that they understand the need to develop people, but they don't know how to do it. It seems to be either complicated, time-consuming, or both. I want to offer a simple plan that will help you. Think of it as a lattice framework that gives some supporting structure for the people to grow and develop. You have the freedom to add, modify, and direct it as much as you need to meet the demands of your specific business. Let's dive in.

Recruiting.

The development of people starts at the beginning, even before they become part of your team. Find the best people that you can to fill the positions you have. This involves clearly knowing what opportunity is available in your business. What responsibilities are vital for success? What skills are needed? What qualities *must* the person have (minimum), and what qualities does *an ideal* person possess (an all-star). Now, you are crystal clear on what kind of person you are looking for.

Let me give an example with our recruiting process in our clinics. Let's say that we are growing, and we need to add another administrative/receptionist position. We have clearly identified what specific responsibilities this new role will have and what an ideal candidate would be. This allows us to go through the initial number of resumes that come in, and we take our top candidates through our interviewing process. This begins with the candidate meeting with an office manager. The first thing the candidate gets is a sheet that has our clinic mission and our core convictions. The office manager explains these are what we are about and what is important along the way. And she is looking to see the candidate's response to this. If their eyes light up, and they engage in meaningful questions and conversations about them, then they can move on to other parts of the interview. If they have the greatest skills in the world but could care less about the mission and core convictions, they are not a fit for our team. If the manager believes the candidate should move on in the process, another interview is scheduled with the team leader of the admin team. The first part of that interview is to pull another copy of the mission and core values and say, "This is how our specific department works together to complete the mission of the clinic." By consistently reinforcing what the mission and convictions of your business are, it allows those candidates that want to share in them rise to the top. It also keeps your existing team reminded of what the business is all about.

Positioning.

Put your team in the best position to win. Allow people to work as much as possible in the area of their strengths. As your business grows and changes, the people also grow and change. Place them in a position that best fits with these growing demands and changes.

Example.

Show others the fleshing out of the mission. Show them expressions of your core convictions. Be an example of influence, impact, and encouragement.

Equipping.

Give your team what they need to do their *jobs* well—training, tools, opportunities, etc. Create a culture in which people want to get better at their responsibilities and then provide what is needed to get them there.

Enlarge.

Help others in their lives by providing materials, books, conferences, mentoring, and opportunities to develop them as people.

Empower.

Give them increasing responsibilities and opportunities to succeed. Empowered people can be the most vital component to your business success. They get the vision. They understand what needs to be done to accomplish it. They are highly skilled in their area of responsibility, and they are fully engaged. They make things happen. But getting people to this stage does not happen naturally. It takes attention, focus, and effort on your part. Here is the road to engagement:

1. **Training:** showing and telling them what needs to be done

2. **Mentoring:** working alongside them while they are doing what needs to be done

3. **Coaching:** occasionally checking on them as they are working independently and asking questions concerning their progress, successes, difficulties, and what they need to get better

4. **Delegating:** releasing them to take on significant responsibilities to make the business grow and succeed. This is a sweet spot for them as they are experiencing a deeper sense of satisfaction and fulfillment with their work, but this is a great place for you as an owner. You are developing people. You are impacting their lives in a profound manner. Your satisfaction and fulfillment are also growing. And the more of these people you have in your business, then the better your business will be.

Resources

Now that we understand the importance of people, let's move on to the **resources** we have or those we need to get. As we go through this, keep in mind that resources are a vital part of your *mission,* one that's purpose is to fulfill, carry out, and accomplish your *vision* for the business. You may be in the very early stages of starting your business and just developing some of these resources. Some of you may not even have any at this time, but you will as you grow. As you are creating and developing these resources, keep in mind this question: "How will this resource *best accomplish the vision I have for this business?*"

Others of you have been in the game for a number of years, and you have some systems, policies, and departments that have existed for quite a while. Steward them. Make the most of them. Are they currently best-suited to accomplish the vision you have? Can they be tweaked, modified, overhauled, thrown away, or enhanced to best get you where you believe you are being called by God to lead your business? Don't fall into the common church paradigm that says, "Well, we've always done it this way!"

Five Missional Departments

There is a Pentathlon of Life, and there is a Pentathlon of Business Mission. These are five departments that are the backbone of your business. Early in your business, it is like you are the parent of five little kids. You are the one that is doing the work for all of them. As your business grows, these little departments will grow and mature, soon able to accomplish their tasks with very little input from you.

Sales and Marketing.

Earlier you answered questions about what you do or produce, who you serve, and what those you serve value. This is the part of your business that is responsible for finding those people and telling them your story. Not some sensationalized fictional tale that comes across like a high school Facebook post, pretending to appear as something you are not. It may bring customers in initially, but they will not stay because they smell a bait and switch. Character and integrity are not to be part of your life, but they permeate through all of your life, including through your business and the story you tell about your business.

Remember, there is an abundance of people looking for what you are and what you do. Tell *your* story so those who are looking for what you are providing can find you and taste and see that what you provide is indeed good.

Operations.

This is what creates and delivers what you do. There is a multitude of ways to do this, but again, are you doing it in a way that best accomplishes the mission of fulfilling the vision for the business? Do your policies enhance or slow down the mission? Are your procedures best accomplishing what needs to be done? Hint: The people closest to the frontlines of operations can have the best insights on what is going on and what needs to be done to improve. By consistently asking them, "How can we get better at what we are doing?" you not only get some of the clearest information available, but it makes them feel more a part of the mission and vision of the business. They become a much more engaged employee. That's a win-win situation.

Finances.

This is overseeing all the fuel of the business. All the money that comes in, goes out, what remains, and what you plan to do with it. Before we talk about how to handle the money, let's make sure that we understand the nature of money. Money is amoral. This means that it's neither inherently good nor bad. Money does not corrupt or make you righteous. However, money does *reveal*. It reveals our hearts to everyone who is watching. Money does not cause someone to become greedy, materialistic, or corrupt. They already are, and an increase in cash flow gives them the opportunity to show it off.

When you look in the Bible you will see four kinds of people concerning money and their hearts:

- Righteous and rich
- Righteous and poor
- Unrighteous and rich
- Unrighteous and poor

So which category would you put yourself in? Which one would your customers, employees, spouse, and children put you in? What category do you want to be in?

Money is also quite important—kind of like oxygen. If it is not available, there is a pretty good chance that your business will die. No money, no business. No money, no ministry. While we do not worship money, we should not disregard its importance. Did you know that the Bible refers to money about 2,000 times? There are also about 500 verses that refer to faith. The same is true for prayer. This certainly is not to say that money is more important than faith or prayer. That's stupid. It certainly would indicate that God has a great deal to say about money because it is important.

Money is morally neutral, reveals the heart, and has some importance. It is also a tool. Finances allow you to build something. Produce something. Create something. And the reality is that if we have more tools, we can build more useful and beneficial things. Remember what I said to the Moldavian dentist earlier?

"Who said that this is all for you?"

A shop full of tools can be used to build more useful and beneficial things than a tiny Plano toolbox sitting in the corner of your garage. Good stewardship is getting tools and building in a way that honors God and benefits others.

If your business is small, you are the CFO of the business. You deposit the checks, pay the bills, do the payroll, and work on budgets. As your business grows, other people begin to take some of the responsibilities. You get an accountant, someone to oversee money coming in, and someone else paying the overhead.

Let's talk about two important points to remember as you grow. One, get help and do not do this all on your own. The less time you are focused on these tasks, the more time you can spend leading and growing your business. Second, get multiple people involved in this. The more skillful people involved, brings a greater level of accountability to the accounting.

So money is morally neutral, reveals the heart, is important, and is a useful tool. Now, do you have a plan for it? How does your budget and cash flow work to get your business from where it currently is to where you want it to go? You know, the vision and what God is calling you to do? To make the best use of the financial tools that come to you is to have a clear and solid understanding of what to do with them. The vision. The mission. This utilizes the finances in the most beneficial way and decreases the chances of doing something wasteful or stupid with it.

Human Resources (HR).

HR encompasses recruiting and hiring new employees, overseeing benefits and compensation, performance management and reviews, as well as HR data and analytics. To be honest, just writing this down makes my stomach upset. I can't stand this stuff. However, there are some people who absolutely love this. Find that person and spend time with them so they absolutely get your vision for the business. Train them. mentor them. Coach them. Delegate this to them. Then continue to spend some time with them to help them become the best they can be. This person or team becomes a significant bridge between the owner and the whole team. Therefore, they must eat the vision for breakfast to help the team carry it out the mission to get there.

Leadership.

This is your baby. This is your focus. We will get into so much more about leadership in the next section. Leadership is about taking responsibility. Our fallen human condition prefers to focus on authority, call all the shots, and be in charge. Leadership is taking the *responsibility* for stewardship in the business and making the most of the people, resources, and opportunities they are in charge of. It is character on display, moving through skills and service to influence and impact others in pursuing the vision. If someone is a leader of a department, they are to take responsibility for that department in the pursuit of the vision. As your business grows, so will the need for people to take leadership responsibility for certain aspects of the business. As the owner, your great responsibility is to lead the leaders—to impact and influence those that have influence and impact on the business. As your business grows, your focus becomes smaller (number of people) so that your business impact can become even greater.

Opportunities

The mission of the business is to accomplish the vision. Getting from where the business is to where you want it to go. It is stewardship on a larger scale that grows the people and resources. It also makes the most of the **opportunities** that continually appear.

Once again, we see the tremendous value of connecting our faith with our business. When we understand what God is calling us to do, and it manifests itself into a vision for the business, it allows for a great lens to evaluate all the opportunities, choices, options, and events that come up. Clear vision actually eliminates options and opportunities while speeding up decision-making. This means better and more quality decisions are made and acted on. This is being efficient, effective, and productive.

For example, say an opportunity comes up for your business to expand into another location, take on a partner, or dive into a new market. Does it help to accomplish the vision or not? If not, even though it seems like a good opportunity, you pass and move on. It may be great for someone else, but for you, it is not a proper fit. However, if the opportunity greatly enhances the vision, then do it. Yes, vet it properly but your vision has been vetted for years and you know what fits and what does not. If it fits, then jump on it and keep moving forward.

Decision-making can be stressful. It's part of taking responsibility. *Do not* disregard the value of the Holy Spirit giving wisdom and discernment in seeking answers and direction in your business. After all, didn't He call you to something? Didn't He give you a vision for the business interests that you have? Of course. But He didn't just initiate these things, He wants to be intimately involved in them. Do you need wisdom? You better believe it! Could you use some clear insights into what is right and wrong, noble or foolish, valuable or counterfeit? He's there for the asking. More importantly, He's here for everything.

Having a business mission is a topic that is discussed extensively in the business community. For many, it becomes nothing more than a plaque on the wall and a pithy saying. And that is about as effective as it gets. Nothing more than some words on the wall that some can recite but none are impacted by.

But you can be different. God has given you a vision and placed within you a burning desire to bring it to life. What could be, should be. What can be, must be. That's your mission for your business.

You are not building just any business. Your business interests are mission-critical.

God is making you into a solution for a problem that needs to be fixed. You were made for this.

Chapter Nine

BUSINESS TOOLS TO GET THE JOB DONE

Your business vision answers the questions "Why does the business exist?" and "Where are we going?" Your business mission answers, "How do we accomplish this?" Business tools answer "What do we need to get the job done?"

Tools are important to get the job done, whether it's for building an office space or the business that will be operating inside of it. As a business leader, you will need a number of proper tools to lead your business along its mission to accomplish the vision.

And the choices that are available are as numerous as the stars, each claiming to be the next "must-have" to make your business run faster, more efficiently, more profitably, etc. As a result, business leaders wind up purchasing too many tools—or even unnecessary tools. We are like the husband who tells his wife that he needs to run to Home Depot to pick up *one* thing. Who comes out of Home Depot with only one thing? Yet, the way we go about our home projects is very similar to how we run our businesses.

Most business leaders come into a business coaching relationship seeking a tool to help them solve a problem they are experiencing. They are seeking a time management tool to help them schedule their day. They need help with organizing the workflow on their desk or a template on how to run more effective meetings. But getting them the correct tool right away is not the best thing to do. Many times, it can be harmful.

If you are building furniture, you don't need a welding blow torch. If you are doing automotive repair, then a table saw won't cut it (pun intended).

Selecting a proper business tool comes out of knowing exactly what you are building. You are building a business that has a mission that fulfills a vision and calling, which finds its place in the Pentathlon of your Life and the Priority of One. It's vital that our decision process begins at the top and works its way down. Start with a vision . . . then your mission . . . then the tools to best accomplish it all.

It sounds so simple, yet it is easy to get off track. In every industry, the primary focus is on tools and not the mission. How many marketing efforts are trying to get you to purchase a product yet never ask you about your vision or mission? How many conferences, trade shows, events, or vendors have bombarded you with information about great working tools, yet never ask about your specific vision and mission?

Let me give you an example from my experience. When we were going to build our existing clinic, I hired an architect to help design it. This guy was unbelievable. He was not only a licensed architect, but he was also a dentist, and his firm specialized in only designing dental offices. During one of our initial visits, he asked me all sorts of questions about how we functioned as a clinic so he could design the facility to best enhance how we functioned. He asked if I wanted a private office. I told him I did. He asked if in my private office if I wanted a private bathroom as well. I told that would be great. Then he wanted to know if I wanted a shower in my bathroom. I told him I didn't really see the need for one. He said, "Good because I would have done my best to talk you out of getting one. Too many times the shower becomes the storage place for all of the latest techno-gadgets that dentists buy and wind up not using."

I'm certain that you have similar stories in your specific industries. Too many of us buy tools that really don't serve the mission well, and they wind up just taking up space. They not only waste space, but they also waste a lot of cash that could be put to better use.

Always keep in the front of your mind what exactly it is you are building; then, you will be able to select the best business tools to accomplish the mission.

There are a couple of tools I want to bring up that will benefit you as a business leader regardless of what industry you are in.

KPI Dashboard

KPI stands for *key performance indicators*. These are the key areas of your business you can measure that gauge progress and performance of how the business is doing. KPI acts like the dashboard of a car that tells you some critical information about how the car is doing.

What are just five areas of your business you can measure that will tell you how your business is doing? What are the vital signs of your business that will tell you—quickly—if things are healthy, growing, or need attention? What these indicators are will be unique to your business because they reveal how the business is doing in accomplishing your business mission.

Let me share with you what our KPIs are for our clinics:

- How many new patients are scheduled for today?
- How many patients were seen yesterday and left with their next appointment scheduled and confirmed?
- How many patients, who were scheduled yesterday, missed or failed their appointment?
- Who are the patients that are scheduled to see us today who have a previously diagnosed condition and whose treatment has not been scheduled yet?

That's it. This is shared with everyone at the morning huddle to start the day, and we track it through the day and record it. It is simple to do, and for us, these are the best indicators of how we are doing on a daily basis. If we do these things really well, then so many other things fall into place. If these numbers begin to go south, it immediately lets us know there is some aspect of the business that needs to be looked into . . . *now*.

You can certainly measure other things. Good information is critical for leading your business. Several years ago, we hired a practice management consulting group to help up with our clinic. They had us track, measure, and report on all sorts of areas. Weekly and monthly, we were given graphs, charts, and impressive-looking reports. Now, I really don't need much help to realize that I can be stupid, and going over mountains of data was only making the case against me more evident. When everything we measure is important, what gets lost is what is *vital* to the business. Just like in a medical situation, the doctor wants to know what the *vital* signs of the patient are. By looking at those vital signs the doctor gets a quick understanding of what the status of the patient is and what needs to be looked at *pronto* or if other tests need to be done first.

I'm not saying only measure a few things, but what are the key indicators that you want to see every day to know the health of the business? This is like looking at the dashboard of a jet airliner compared to your car. The jet has numerous gauges, dials, buttons, and monitors, and they all serve a purpose. Your car has gas, battery, oil pressure, and most importantly your Bluetooth to play your favorite music or podcast. You can measure all you want and read as many reports as you want, but what is *vital* to know? What will give you an indication about whether you need to look into some area of your business to make changes to enhance and improve getting the mission done?

How do you know what metric is vital to your business? How do you determine what metrics should go onto your dashboard? Here are two helpful questions to ask yourself:

1. **What is one metric that if you focused to improve, would have the greatest impact on your business?** That one definitely needs to be on there and looked at every day with an action plan to improve it.

2. **What is your 80/20?** I'm sure that you have heard of the Pareto Principle, or as it's commonly known as, the "80/20 Rule," This is the observation that 80 percent of the outcomes result from 20 percent of the causes. This is seen in 80 percent of church giving comes from 20 percent of the people; 80 percent of your sales come from 20 percent of your products; 80 percent of your employee problems probably come from only 20 percent of your employees. You get the idea. So, what is your 20 percent that results in your 80 percent? What are those metrics that indicate the real strength of your business? Those few things that really give you your best results. Get those on your dashboard as well. Then, focus on how you can make them even better! If 20 percent of your products, services, or efforts are yielding 80 percent of the results that you want, then make sure that you are spending 80 percent of your time, effort, and resources on that 20 percent!

Your business environment is fluid. There are many factors and numerous influences that cause change. A dashboard will be a great tool for you to have so you can know the changes that are occurring and make the necessary quick adjustments to keep your business on mission. This will help it continue to grow in a healthy, stable, and positive way.

KPI Meetings

This is "Keep People Informed through various meetings." The reason we have meetings is to communicate important information. What type of meeting, who is part of the meeting, or how frequently you have meetings is totally up to you. The key is to understand what the purpose of the meeting is. Do not have meetings just for the sake of having meetings. It may sound impressive to have numerous meetings, but it could also be an indication that you are wasting a lot of time and resources.

I was having a casual talk with another business owner a few years ago. He shared with me that he had just finished Jim Collins' book, *Good to Great*, and his takeaway from the book was that great businesses have meetings. So he started having meetings in his business.

"What kind of meetings are you having, and what is the purpose you have for them?" I asked.

"Well, we're having them because we want to become great," he responded.

A swing and a miss.

Having meetings for the sake of having meetings is like having tools that you either don't know how to use or are unnecessary.

Meetings are certainly necessary because communication is necessary. It's vital. Lack of communication is one of the major frustrations common to all organizations, whether it is a business, a church, a non-profit, or within our families. As the business owner or leader, it is your responsibility to make sure that communication happens.

How do you best communicate with others? Do you like to talk, or do you prefer to write using email or an office-wide chat program? Use the communication style that you are most comfortable with and embrace it. The more comfortable you feel with it, the more likely you will use it. And believe me, you need to communicate with your team. Many notes, memos, reports, and announcements can be sent digitally, with the option to respond. Technology is a great tool, so use it to the advantage of your business.

Group Meetings

There are times when there is a need for a meeting with other people. Whether the people get together through Zoom or in person, there are some helpful guidelines to consider so you can make the most out of your meeting (yep, stewardship once again!).

- **Schedule it.** By scheduling a meeting, it stresses that it's important. If it is a recurring meeting, then schedule it out for the next quarter or through the year. Here is a suggestion for understanding how important your meeting is: When you have a meeting with various people in your business, you are pulling them away from their usual business activities that are moving the business forward. Let's say you are going to meet for one hour. Add up one hour of payroll for every individual attending that meeting. That's a little insight as to the financial cost of having the meeting. Make sure what you cover is worth more than the salary investment. See, meeting just for the sake of meeting is quite costly. And wasteful.

- **Have an agenda.** Let people know what the meeting is going to be about. Let them prepare mentally so they can participate and bring as much value to the meeting as possible. If there are issues to be discussed, let them know ahead of time so they have time to think and are ready to go. Have you ever been in a meeting and asked a question and the response from others is, "That's a great question. I'm gonna have to think about that one." Let them think about it before the meeting rather than during or after the meeting.

- **Have a set starting time and an ending time.** Starting on time lets people know the meeting is important. Ending on time lets them know you value their time, and they are important. Having an ending time prevents from getting off track and wasting time. If a topic does come up that does have some urgency or importance but is not the focus of the current meeting, simply acknowledge it and put it on an agenda for another time.

- **If decisions need to be made, then make sure a consensus is reached and everyone is committed to the decision.** I would highly recommend Patrick Lencioni's book, *The 5 Dysfunctions of a Team*. I have taken every doctor, office manager, team leader, and entire clinic teams through this book. I have given it to the pastoral team I am a part of, and I keep numerous extra copies to give to other business owners that meet with me. I cannot recommend it enough in helping organizational teams work at their very best.

- **Finish well.** At the end of every meeting, spend just a few moments giving a recap. If a decision was reached, then what was committed to? If assignments or tasks were given, then who committed to doing them? One thing I like to end meetings with is by asking this question: "What was the most important or profitable thing you personally got out of our time together?" Everyone must answer. What they say is extremely valuable. It will give you insights into what they really value. They may value the decisions that were made or the clarity that was given. You will be able to gain insights on how to make your meetings even better. It is feedback you can really benefit from.

One-on-One Meetings

Meeting with individuals on a one-on-one basis is one of the most valuable uses of your time for your business. As pointed out earlier, people are your most valuable resource. Their development and growth will have an incredible impact on your business. A simple outline for developing people is to start out with training them, then mentor them, and then we move on to coaching them and delegating them to take on some responsibility on their own. This is what I refer to as "letting good things run wild." Many businesses start with training. Very few make it to delegating. The most common reason why it falls apart is that the leader does not invest the time needed to develop others.

One-on-one meetings with others amplifies communication. As a result, it amplifies impact.

1. **Employees feel a greater sense of being valued.** Being part of a group meeting allows the participants to feel valued as part of a team. Meeting one-on-one with the business leader puts that sense of value on steroids.

2. **Relational trust increases.** Trust is a foundational building block for teams to function well and get the results needed for the business. One-on-one meetings allow a relationship between the employee and leader to grow and deepen. Trust builds. Commitment deepens. Engagement increases. Great results show up.

3. **Greater development.** This is a time when leaders can coach others by asking some probing questions that are extremely beneficial. Here are some suggestions:

   - What has gone really well since we last met together?
   - What factors played a key role in this?
   - What are the current challenges you are facing?
   - What have you done to overcome these challenges?
   - What are the next steps you need to take in our mission?
   - What do you need to accomplish this?
   - What can I do to help and support you?

It's a simple process of gaining a clear understanding of where things are right now (reality), where things need to go (mission to accomplish vision), and what needs to be done to get there (clear next steps of development, growth, and impact). Asking these questions is not an interrogation but tools to help a business leader really shepherd and grow the people who have been placed under their care. Make a commitment to these people. Make the time for them. Get this on the schedule because it is that important, and when you meet with them, make them the focus of your time together.

4. **The vision gets clearer and the mission more focused.** During these meetings, the application of the vision and mission becomes clearer for the employee. They become even more mission-focused. That influence then moves out into their areas of responsibility to impact others. As the business leader or owner, you are not the sole spokesman of the vision and mission. Others are catching it and spreading it. More are embracing it. And then you start to actually see it in the daily workings of the business. All this happens because you chose to invest your time in the strategic people in your business and help them develop in ways they could not do by themselves. You are seeing good things running wild!

Time Management Tools and Other Deceitful Lies

There is an abundance of tools that claim to help with time management. None of them work. Why? Because we cannot manage time. Managing and directing time is one of the items on God's to-do list. It is way over all of our paygrades. We can't start time, stop time, or even impact time. What we can do is manage ourselves as we go through time. Maybe you think that I'm just splitting hairs over this, but hear me out. Far too many business owners and leaders believe that if they could just find the right calendar, watch, software, system, or desk arrangement template, then they would be more productive, disciplined, and motivated. But issues of discipline, motivation, and productivity are really issues of the heart. That's where they begin, at least. The new calendar will not make you more disciplined if you have not already determined in your heart to be more disciplined. If you're not motivated, new software or a template isn't going to get you there. Too many are blaming their heart issues on tools. Proper tools in the hands of a wise and skillful leader can be quite powerful.

> *Therefore, be careful how you walk, not as unwise men, but as wise, making the most of your time because the days are evil. (Ephesians 5:15–16)*

Again, you cannot manage time, but you can manage yourself as you go through time. That's what the wise do in making the most of their time. It's your time. It's been given to you from the God who is in charge of time. So make the most of it (stewardship again!).

Here is a suggestion on how to connect a time-focused tool with your vision and calling on your business so that you can make the most of it.

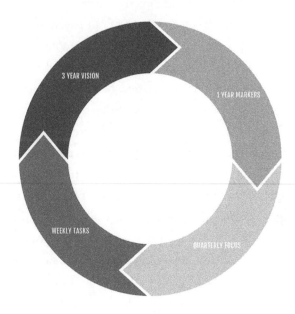

This allows you to number your days and make the most of your time based upon your vision for the business. It helps keep the vision consistently in front of you and focuses all of your efforts to move in that direction. Wouldn't you love to have the clarity and confidence to know that what you are doing on Tuesday of this week will have a meaningful effect three years later!

Three-year vision: You already know what your vision for your business looks like. You can describe it in vivid detail. In this box, write down what your vision looks like in three years. What are revenues like? How is the culture different? What are the customers' or clients' experiences? What impacts have been made? Write them down. I like a three-year timeframe because one year is too short for significant change to occur, and five years seems too far away and diminishes urgency. What if your vision for your business is more than three years out? Not a problem. Just ask yourself what your ten-year vision will look like in three years.

One-year markers: When you are pursuing a three-year vision, what will it look like after one year? What does it need to look like after one year? Are you on track? What is happening after one year for you to be satisfied with the progress you are making? If you are not satisfied, what changes need to be made? It is important to make these markers as tangible as possible so you can definitively answer yes or no as far as accomplishing them.

Quarterly focus: You have a three-year vision. You have laid out clear goals for the next year to accomplish that vision. Now, take the next three-month quarter and lay out one to three key projects for the business to focus on that will help accomplish a one-year goal. What needs to be changed? What needs to be initiated or introduced? What specific work needs to be done to accomplish the goals that make the vision a reality? Hint: Wishful thinking and dreaming about it doesn't work. Also, share this with your entire team. They love to have a focus for their daily work routines. They love to see the positive changes within a ninety-day period. They love to see that their work really matters.

Let me give you a personal example. Two years ago, we noticed the number of patients failing or canceling their appointments was starting to increase. We made correcting this an emphasis for the next three months. People shared all sorts of ideas on how to improve this. We talked about it in our morning huddle, staff meetings, and leaders' meetings. We agreed on new and better habits and procedures that would add value to the patients' visits and express the importance of their next visit. We tracked the numbers and watched as this specific area of the clinic improved tremendously. Here is one of the best parts: As we moved to a new area to focus on for the next ninety days, the new habits, procedures, and improvements developed during the previous days continued and remain with us today. They didn't revert back to what they once were. Good became great . . . and great decided to stay and become the norm.

Weekly tasks: You have a vision. You have laid out what that should look like one year from now. You have come up with specific projects and areas to focus on for the next ninety days that will accomplish those goals. Now, you have a much clearer focus on the tasks that must be done during the week. Sure, there are many things that go on your weekly calendar, but not all tasks carry the same impact and value for your business. Check to make sure that the most important tasks are getting your time and attention. Remember that you have a team that has been developed (train-mentor-coach-delegate) so they can take on certain tasks so you are not doing everything; most everything is being accomplished by others. You are invested in those vital things that have your attention today so impactful results are showing up this year, and a vision will become a reality in three years. You are truly numbering your days and making the most of your time. The importance of tomorrow is being prepared today.

May I offer a suggestion at this time? When you get to Friday, or the end of your workweek, look at the tasks and activities that were accomplished. Realize that you moved the ball downfield. Take time to celebrate that. Take time to specifically thank God for those things. They are not insignificant. They are steps in the journey you are taking as you respond to the calling that God has given you.

You will probably find that your faith is growing deeper.

Your business is actually getting better.

There is a growing satisfaction and fulfillment in you that escapes too many in the world of business.

You are ready to move on and enjoy your weekend.

And you can't wait for Monday!

SECTION THREE
GREATER IMPACT

The Quest for Authentic and Impactful Leadership

A compass that points straight back at you—like a life mission that is only about serving yourself- is a useless tool that will take you precisely nowhere. Leadership over time is far more difficult than orienteering or even vacationing, yet we often approach it with less forethought than we do a week at the beach.

Donovan Campbell, former captain, United States Marines

	PREPARATION	PRODUCTION	PROVISION	POWERFUL PRIVILEGE
PRIMARY RESPONSIBILITY	PREPARATION	PRODUCTION	PROVISION	POWERFUL PRIVILEGE
PRIMARY FOCUS	**YOU**	**YOUR TEAM**	**YOUR ORGANIZATION**	**YOUR COMMUNITY**
LEADERSHIP DEVELOPMENT AND INFLUENCE	**POSITION** ↘ **RELATIONAL**	**RELATIONAL** ↘ **PRODUCTIVE**	**PRODUCTIVE** ↘ **PEOPLE**	**PEOPLE** ↘ **POWERFUL INFLUENCE**
WHAT IS BEING GAINED	Personal growth through knowledge, understanding and discernment	Wisdom and skill through sacrifice, scripture, shaping, shepherding, stewardship	Multiplication of desired results due to delegation and strategic giving of time, resources, and acquired wisdom	An incredible sense of responsibility and satisfaction that few get to experience. Longing to hear, "well done, good and faithful servant"
CALLING DEVELOPMENT AND TRANSITION	**FORMING**	**FOCUSING**	**FINISHING STRONG**	**FINALIZING**
DESCRIPTION	**DISCERNING**	**DIFFICULT**	**DESIRES & DANGERS**	**DOMINANT**

Gaining a heart of wisdom...

as we number our days...

Chapter Ten

LEADERSHIP AS A WAY OF LIFE

uilding and growing a healthy and productive business is best accomplished with a sound theological foundation and guidance. It also requires good leadership that influences and impacts people along the way. There is so much that has been written about leadership in recent years, and there appears to be no end in sight. As Solomon wrote in Ecclesiastes, "But beyond this my son, be warned: the writing of books is endless, and excessive devotion to books is wearying to the body." Can I get an "Amen" on that!

I love to read, and one of my favorite topics is leadership. I have shelves filled with books in our study at home, a huge assortment on my Kindle app on my phone, and shelves and boxes of them at work that I hand out to others. Many of them are great. Some have been deleted from my phone after one reading or thrown into the trash.

I intend to present to you a leadership matrix, or grid, that allows you to better understand leadership, influence, and impact as you grow through various seasons of your business and life. As you grow, mature, and change, so does your business. Your leadership does as well. As you, your business, and your leadership grow through these seasons we will answer some critical questions such as:

- What are the primary characteristics of these various seasons?

- Who is the primary focus of my leadership? Who needs to be impacted the most?

- What is changing during these various seasons of leadership?

- What is happening that signals a transition from one season to the next?

- What is happening to me, as well as the business, during these seasons?

Having this leadership matrix in your head will allow you to sift through the mounds of information on leadership and place it in the best position as it applies to *you* and *where you are* at present.

Before we dive into what good leadership is, let's take a look at a few of the common myths about leadership that are flat-out wrong.

One-Size-Fits-All Leadership

Nope. Not even close. Life is too dynamic and changing. You and your business are dynamic and changing. One static and fixed style of leadership will not be effective enough through life. The focus of someone leading a small startup business is not the same as one who is leading a thirty-year-old business that has steadily grown over the years.

Several years ago, I was going to be seen in the Orthopedic department for an evaluation of my lower back. I was about four years removed from my days as an offensive lineman at the University of Iowa. I had slimmed down to my current six-foot-three-inch, 240-pound size. As I was sitting in an examination room, a nurse came in and told me that I would need to take off my cloths, put them in a bag, and then put on a hospital gown. The package on the gown said, "One size. Fits all."

It should have said, "One size. Fits most sixth graders."

It may have been a tight fit, but at the least, it was really short on me.

Then the nurse came back in and informed me they were very busy, and they needed to move me to another place so they could use that examination room. The other room they moved me to was the waiting room. A very full waiting room.

Did I mention that all my clothes were in a bag, and I was wearing a kid's robe with nothing on underneath?

"One size fit all" is not true for hospital gowns. It's also not true in leadership. To believe it is true for leadership may result in a great deal of embarrassment. Believe me, I know.

"One-size-fits-all" leadership also doesn't work in my home. I don't lead, influence, and impact my seventeen-year-old son, who is a senior in high school, drives a car, and is preparing to leave the home in one more year the same way I do my four-year-old that can't zip up his pants, tie his shoes, and still has training wheels on his bike. Treat a seventeen-year-old young man like he is four, and he will not respect or honor you while he is looking forward to the day he can leave. Give a four-year-old the freedom and responsibility of a seventeen-year-old, and you might find your house on fire.

Everyone Is a Leader. Anyone Can Lead.

Nope. Again, not even close. Some people are great at leading, impacting, and influencing people. Others just plain suck at it. Just look at some people in politics or running some businesses. Look at some pastoral team leading churches. Look at some of the homes in your neighborhood. Poor leadership is on display in every facet of our world. Not everyone can lead well. However, some people make great followers. They prefer it. Followers can be loyal. They can also be lazy. Support and keep your loyal followers in your business because they are a tremendous asset. Lazy ones tend to be a pain in the asset. Let the lazy ones have the honor of working somewhere else.

Leadership is Easy and Comes Naturally.

Want to know what really comes easy and naturally? Breakdown. Stagnation. Chaos. You do not have to work at all to have this trinity show up in your business. Just give it time, and they will come around like weeds do in a garden. Real effective leadership requires focus and effort. It requires change and growth. It will be developed through time, pressure, and trial. Leadership is hard. Great leadership is really hard. Yet, it is so worth it!

The world has enough poor leadership that is empty, selfish, and lazy. Leadership that relies only on titles and positions but still can't zip up its pants and needs training wheels to take on the slightest of responsibility is all too common.

But not you.

You have a desire to take on responsibility and make the most of the people, opportunities, and resources that sit before you. You want to impact and influence the people around you and make them better. You want to let God transform you in such a way that you bring a beneficial influence and impact into all the areas that He places you in. That's what can happen when one deeply connects their faith with their business interests.

Ben is a guy like that. He really wants to connect his faith with his business interests. Ben is going to be our avatar as we travel through these seasons of leadership and impact. An avatar is a figure that represents a particular person. It's also the title of a pretty good movie, but for our sake, we will stick with Ben representing a person. Maybe watch the movie later.

Seasons of Life and Leadership

Psalm 90 is known as a prayer of Moses. In it are a couple of verses that serve as a condensed version of a life plan:

1. Verse 10 says that we can anticipate a life span of seventy to eighty years. We are not guaranteed to live

that long, but it's true for most people. Those years can be summarized as toil and trouble. They will also seem to pass by quickly. Not exactly "your best life now" kind of stuff, but this is the Bible speaking, so it's best to stick with it.

2. Verse 11 says that few factor in the reality of God over these years.

3. Verse 12 is asking God to give us a heart of wisdom throughout all of our days.

What does wisdom look like as it's rolled out day after day over seventy to eighty years? What does wisdom look like in someone leading a business and wanting to number his days over a lifetime? I believe that looking at our lives moving through various seasons can provide some much-needed insight. Take a look at Ecclesiastes 3:1, 10–11:

> To everything there is a season, a time for every purpose under heaven. I have seen the task which God has given the sons of men with which to occupy themselves. He has made everything appropriate in its time.

Life goes through various seasons. Take a look at the natural progression of a man. He starts out as a child. Eventually, he becomes a young man. Soon afterward, he becomes a husband. Then a dad. Some years later, he is grandpa.

During these seasons, there is also a progression of the roles and responsibilities, which he takes on. As a child, he is learning to lead himself. His primary responsibility is his preparation and training. He spends a great deal of time in school and mows some yards during the summer so that someday, he can buy his first used car. The young man is almost done with college and works part-time at Home Depot selling lawn mowers. He realizes soon enough, he will be moving into a time of leading more than just himself. The husband and dad is now leading some more than just himself. He has a wife and kids. He wants to purchase his high school daughter her first used car. Actually, he would prefer something like a tank so if she does wind up in an accident, she comes out on top. He is also teaching his younger son the art of lawn mowing and that the new baseball glove his son wants is only five mowed lawns away. Grandpa is in a season of great influence. He is an elder at his church and has owned a car dealership in the community. He has made a great number of significant relationships over the years, and his focus is on the local church and community.

This is a natural and normal progression of life. Thankfully, life has a way of gradually unfolding one season after another. Therefore, there are some things we can predict. There are some things we can anticipate. There are some things we can plan for.

Four seasons occur over seventy to eighty years. They are the seasons of Preparation, Production, Provision, and Powerful Privilege. Each season progresses over time, and each season requires greater wisdom. That is why Moses prayed for a heart of wisdom throughout his days until the end of his life. We should do no less.

Here are some characteristics of these seasons and their progression:

1. Each season has many opportunities to be involved in, but it also has one primary obligation that is foremost.

2. This primary obligation is vital to fulfilling the roles and responsibilities of the season we currently find ourselves in.

3. The primary obligation is a key stepping stone to function effectively in the next season.

4. By not anticipating or properly planning for the next season, this may cause you to enter in unprepared or go through the next season greatly unfulfilled.

5. Whatever season you find yourself in, God has something important for you to do.

6. Throughout our lives God is not only using us where we are but also continually preparing us for something that needs to be done.

7. The sad reality is that very few make it to the end with a heart of wisdom after numbering their days. So let us make the needed steps to stay off that casualty list and reach the end and His proclamation of, "Well done good and faithful servant." What a way to live!

**Time is God's way of making sure
everything does not happen all at once.**

**Wisdom is God's way of making sure that everything that
needs to be done can happen properly and effectively.**

**We can have the opportunity to do everything
we need to do—one season at a time.**

Remember, to "everything there is a season and a time for every purpose under heaven." He has made everything appropriate in its time. It is true in life. It is true in business. It is true in how we lead and impact through seventy to eighty years.

We will look at Ben's life as a fictional example. As we go through his story, put your nonfictional self in his shoes and think about what God has done in your life to prepare you . . . what critical things must be done now and what He is preparing you for in your next season of life, leadership, and business. As you read through this next chapter, you will notice that some of the key terms of each season are emboldened to help identify the trees that make up the forest.

Understanding the unfolding seasons of life and leadership is how we can grow up and not become a screw-up. There are certainly enough of the latter group around us.

There are problems to be solved; solutions to be offered, and people to be impacted. A God to be honored.

Time to be like the men of Issachar, who knew what must be done (1 Chronicles 12:32).

The day of living small has come to an end.

Chapter Eleven

THE SEASONS OF LEADERSHIP

Leadership is something more than a title or position. Leadership is a character trait that not only impacts and influences people, but also produces some really great results. Leadership is best viewed as something that grows and develops through specific seasons over a lifetime, which produces not only great results but also a deep sense of satisfaction and fulfillment.

Let's follow Ben through these various seasons, and let his life serve as an example of leadership development and impact over a lifetime.

The Season of Preparation

The Season of Preparation is the time from the child to the young adult. It is the time when the child is being prepared to be launched into the world as an independent adult, one who will hopefully be a blessing to others rather than a burden. This is a time when leadership is being formed, nurtured, and developed. Ben is nearing the end of this season. He is twenty-one years old and in his final year of college, majoring in business.

Ben came to faith in Christ during his early teens. It is during this season that Ben is becoming **a leader of one.** He is learning to lead **himself.** He is moving from being **self-centered to being self-controlled**. He has learned how to control his anger and emotions. He has a healthy respect for authority and is honoring those around him. He did not need his mama to wake him up for his 11:00 a.m. English class during high school.

Ben is like many other guys in college. He likes to work out a couple of times a week, as well as play pick-up basketball on Saturday mornings. He hangs out with friends, goes to church on Sunday. But with these other activities, he understands that his dominant obligation or priority is his **preparation and training**. He takes his studies seriously. He realizes that this preparation is vital for him to move into his next season of leadership, influence, and impact. If someone cannot lead themselves, how can they be expected to lead others?

This is also a time for Ben to grow in **discernment**. He knows what is noble, truthful, and beneficial, as well as what is foolish, deceitful, and a waste. Even though he is in his early twenties, he has witnessed enough examples of "choices have consequences; you reap what you sow, and nothing good happens right after someone says, 'Here, hold my beer and watch this!'" He also didn't need to look very far because he has his own wins and losses in life, ones born from his choices and their natural consequences.

He was aware of the Law of the Farm and that the relentless pursuit of comfort is indeed the enemy of greatness. You need to prepare the soil and plant in the spring. You need to constantly feed, water, weed, and care for the crop. It's in the fall that there is a harvest and reward. Ben knows of far too many fellow business majors that have a priority of fun and entertainment and then cram for examinations. They gather knowledge but have no understanding. They may get a good grade on the exam, but it will be difficult for them to develop wisdom and skill that benefits others in the arena of business. You can't cram on the farm and expect great results. It doesn't work well in any other place either. That includes in business.

Ben also realizes it is during this time in his life that he is preparing to make some of the most important choices in his life. Some of the choices he will make will impact the quality of his life for the next thirty to forty years. Who will he marry? What kind of work will he pursue? Who will he listen to for advice and direction? What will he seek as a source of truth? How someone is leading themselves during this time will certainly impact what will happen down the road—even forty years down the road.

It was during this season Ben got serious with his faith. It moved from being the faith of his parents and family to *his faith*. He was taking on the responsibility of leading himself. He grew in the understanding of how God made him. Ben had skills, talents, gifts, and desires that were unique to him. Ben greatly appreciated his parents' impact on him while he was in high school because while so many others would ask, "Ben, what do you want to do when you grow up?" it was his parents that would ask, "Ben, what is God calling you to do?" It was this understanding of who he was and the **awakening to God's calling** that brought him to college to study business. It was this calling that also moved him to specifically choose real estate as his career. He was excited that what he was made to do was soon going to be what he was paid to do.

Ben took a position with a large real estate firm in a major market. It was here that he continued in his journey of preparation for leadership development in business. For two years, he watched, learned, observed, listened, and worked his blessed assurance off selling real estate. His calling to the marketplace was awakening and growing. It was becoming clearer and more specific. He was ready to move back to his hometown and open his own real estate business. He felt the excitement, challenge, and passion to integrate his faith with his business.

Ben leased some office space and hired two people for administrative assistance. The calling on his life became the vision for his business. His vision was now taking shape and form. The vision of what "could be" was now on the journey to what "should be."

His time of focused preparation was ending. A new season of leadership and business was upon him. It was time to move from being **a leader of one to a leader of some.**

The Season of Productivity

The Season of Productivity is marked by the growth and productivity of the business.

Ben knew he wanted to steward this business well and make the most out of the people, opportunities, and resources. His leadership influence was in the initial stages, known as **"Title or Positional Leadership."** His two team members really didn't know him very well outside of the recruiting, vetting, and hiring process. They respected Ben, but it was primarily due to his title and position. After all, he was The Boss. The Owner. The Man.

Having influence due to a title or position is a great place to start. Ben had worked extremely hard to get to where he was at. Four years of college. Two years working in the profession. Putting himself on the line to be responsible for a lease, startup costs, and overhead. He definitely earned the position and the title. But he also realized that this was not a place of influence he wanted to stay.

Lots of people start off with a title or position, and they grow beyond that. Those who choose to stay there become dependent on their position alone to influence people. They tend to become proud, arrogant, lazy, and demanding. They become authoritative and exhausting. They are certainly not respected, honored, or admired. They are people of very little influence on the growth, development, and health of the business.

Ben had his share of professors at school, as well as a manager at his first job, to help him realize the sad implications of living in the basement of leadership influence. Again, everyone starts there, but you don't want to settle in for a lifetime.

When Ben wasn't making connections, visiting with clients, or closing on a property, he was making sure he was involved with his team. He repeatedly spoke of the vision and how the team was essential in carrying out the mission. He offered training so they could do their jobs better. He asked questions like, "What do you need to succeed here? What ideas do you have to make us even better? What is something that you see, but I'm missing?"

Ben is moving from **Positional Leadership to Relational Leadership**. He is developing relationships with his team. He is involved. He is giving them needed attention and fostering growth. His team is deepening their trust in him as they see his work ethic and commitment to them and their development on the team. Ben's leadership influence is growing. Because his team appreciates what Ben is doing for them, they are now more engaged in the mission of the business. Communication is clear and ongoing. Office politics and cliques are rare. Trust in each other causes decisions to be made quicker. With a commitment to the mission increasing, the results that the business is striving for are being realized. The business is indeed growing in its productivity and growth. More closings and sales are happening. More revenue in and more expenses going out. The leased space had to be expanded as more people were hired to help with the mission.

However, the business wasn't the only thing that was growing. Ben was being challenged and changed in ways he had never experienced before. No one had told him that this may indeed be the most *difficult* time of his life. Here are some of the common lessons that Ben is going through during this challenging season of leadership development:

- **Stewardship.** It's one thing to read about stewardship. It's a whole different game to actually do it. Intentionally focusing on growing people, resources, and opportunities is hard. With increasing people, resources, and opportunities, it becomes even more difficult. When it's done well, the results are incredible.

- **Squeezing, Shaping, and Sacrifice.** As the great theologian, Mike Tyson, famously said, "Everyone has a great plan until they get punched in the mouth." The term, "bed of roses" is more descriptive of a funeral service than a business. Thorns from the rose bushes are commonly found in the workplace. Isn't that how God described the reality of the workplace to Adam and to all who followed in a broken Creation? Trials, difficulties, and challenges are all a part of work. Ben and his business are no exceptions. When cash is short, he makes sure that his team gets paid first before himself. That's sacrifice. Navigating through a downturn in the economy and when the market gets stagnant—that's being squeezed. Employee turnover and changes, unfulfilled expectations, and dealing with all kinds of people. Shaping is taking place. There are certainly times in a business when the stress gets high. Ben can't worry about it too much right now because it's time to end the workday and head home. Waiting for Ben to get home are his wife and three young children. There are days when Ben feels worn out, beat up, and totally spent at the end of work. At home waits a family that he deeply loves, and he desperately wants to lead them well. Did I mention that this can be a difficult season for business leaders? Ben realizes the most significant time of his day is upon him. It's the first three minutes when he walks in the door at home after work. He knows that two choices are waiting for him. One, he can walk in and let everyone know that he is exhausted and has had a rough day while he heads to the most popular piece of furniture in America, the Lazy-Boy recliner. Emphasis on lazy . . . emphasis on boy. The other choice is to prepare himself to fully engage his family from the moment he sets foot in the door until the time his head hits the pillow hours later.

- **Selfishness.** Nothing quite like some squeezing and the need to sacrifice to help Ben realize some of the deeply ingrained selfishness he has. In dentistry, there is a saying that goes like this: *If you want to see what is in a tube . . . squeeze it!* It's true of people as well. Ben is a man of faith. His allegiance is to Christ. He is forgiven but not perfect. He is being redeemed, transformed, and sanctified, but he is in process and has not arrived. Ben has said some things to his team (and to his wife and children) that he regrets. He also has silent thoughts that he is glad no one hears. Being responsible for a growing business is quite revealing. Selfishness starts to ooze out of the cracks caused by stress. It can also show up during times of abundance. Either way, the source is the same. Ben. Or you and me. This is the reality of the human condition in the world of business. Wherever money and people get together, hearts are on display. The reality for the Christ follower is that forgiveness is real. Change is real. Selfishness can be replaced by *selflessness* as one grows and faith deepens. Keep reading below!

- **Scripture.** Ben realizes that all this squeezing and selfishness is common to all business owners. What is uncommon is Ben's response to it. He has learned *and applied* more biblical truth in his life than ever before. He has moved from having a knowledge of Scripture to becoming a wise and skillful person who is benefiting so many others. Ben is not only growing in his knowledge of Scripture but also in his knowledge of God. Ben's faith is deepening in so many ways. And Ben is not the same man as he was when he first started his business.

- **Shepherding.** This is very similar to stewardship but with one slight modification. Shepherding is becoming more focused on people. Shepherding still desires to make the most of resources and opportunities that one has, but the focus and value of people become heightened. This is what is happening in Ben's life during this time. He has been greatly valued for leading the business in its growth and productivity. His team has increased in size and complexity. They have also increased their trust and loyalty to Ben due to his swelling leadership qualities and influence. Ben's business now has ten agents that work with him, as well as a support team. Ben is still involved with some real estate transactions. His reputation is well known throughout the community, and demand for his services is quite high. However, he is now seeing that instead of just adding to the business impact, it's time to multiply it. To do that, he needs to spend more time developing the people who will become the producers for the business and leaders of influence within the business. This marks a time of transition from this season of leadership to the next season. Ben's calling is becoming more *focused*. It's moved from an awakening call of what *could be* to what *should be*. It is now something more specific, intense, and clear. The initial vision that was cast years ago was now becoming a reality. And Ben was going to make the most of it.

The Season of Provision

As Ben looks back on his Season of Productivity, he reflects on what his own father used to tell him: "The days seem to be so long, yet the years go by so fast." Ben started with a small leased space and two employees. Now, he owns a large office building, and his business now offers residential and commercial real estate services. His family has grown as well. Gone are the days of dance recitals, swimming lessons, and Little League. His oldest is married, two are in college, and one will graduate high school this year. While Ben was building an impressive business, he was also raising a very impressive family. His life plan had always been centered on the fact that an effective *business* plan *must* come out of an effective and dynamic *life* plan. Ben did not seek out to live a balanced life. He committed himself to have a focused life. When at work, he was all there. Every night on his drive home, he would pass that one traffic light where it was his time to pray and thank God for the work that he was able to participate in that day. He would also pray for God to prepare his heart, soul, mind, and strength for when he got home. It was time to engage his family. To love them and lead them. To be all there for them. Then, the next morning on his drive to work, he would pass that same intersection. It was there that he prayed and asked God to prepare his heart, soul, mind, and strength for the business responsibilities that were ahead of him.

The Season of Provision is a time characterized by **giving and providing.** Ben has more discretionary time than he has ever had before. His business has more financial capacity than ever before. He also has gained a heart of wisdom and maturity that he never had before. And Ben is passionately committed to making the best use of all of it.

Ben's focus has moved from just a team of realtors to the entire *organization*. To lead an organization, he has focused himself to primarily **invest in and develop people**. He meets with his direct reports on a weekly basis. He meets with each of them individually once a week as well. He is spending his time **coaching** them by asking many of the same types of questions that he asked when the business was in its infancy. "What do you need to succeed in your part of the mission? What ideas do you have that will help us get to where we need to go? What do you see that I may be missing? What's going well in your department? What obstacles are you facing? What do you need from me that would give you the most benefit right now?"

Ben is also **delegating** to other leaders in the business. Ben knows how to do many things in the organization. So do others. However, there are some things that only Ben can do. That's where his focus lies. Ben has invested a great deal of time, energy, and effort in training, mentoring, and coaching key individuals. When others in the organization are ready, Ben gives them increasing responsibility. He calls it "letting good things run wild!" That's effective delegation. Initially, delegation is with some smaller responsibility that is in their part of the mission. When they are faithful with a little, then they can be trusted with more. And then more. And then even more. It's a biblical premise and effective practice.

Entire departments are now being lead and influenced by others. They have benefited from the leadership influence from Ben over the years. Ben had trained and mentored them. Now, they are the ones who are doing the training and mentoring of so many others in the organization. The vision and influence have multiplied and created a business culture that is committed to individual and organizational growth, as well as providing exceptional service to their clients and their families.

Throughout his career and calling, Ben has watched his leadership influence and impact grow from being a leader of one (himself), moving to a leader of some (his team), to now being a leader of more (the organization). His leadership influence is like a stone thrown into a pond that creates ever-expanding, concentric circles of ripples moving outward. It is the rock-solid clarity of his calling, vision, and stewardship that is the stone making the ever-increasing ripples. It is this calling, vision, and stewardship that is now going to reap even greater benefits in this season of leadership in which he finds himself.

With so many things going well at this time, it is vital to understand that this is a *dangerous* season for many business owners. Many do not navigate it well. When there is more discretionary time, finances are good, and so many others are doing the work of the business, this is when many business owners and executives start to coast. They begin to mentally check out and focus on leisure, recreation, and hobbies instead. Sure, they still come into the office, but the heart, soul, mind, and strength are lacking. At a time when a business is primed for real greatness and impact, too many choose to pursue comfort above everything else. But Ben is different. Ben is serious about his faith. He is serious about stewarding this business. And the integration of these is what makes a huge difference.

Ben has known for a long time that people are a business's most valuable resource. So many business opportunities are driven by relationships and reputation. People bring that to the organization. This is why Ben is now so focused on the key people in his organization, and he is intentional and strategic in spending time with them. This key factor is what differentiates his business from others. He now has the time to do this, and he focuses on it. His competitors on the other hand, either do not have an owner that has the time to invest so much into developing the employees, or if they do have the time, they would rather spend it on pursuing leisure and comfort. This is why other real estate offices do not deliver the same quality of service that Ben's business does.

A deep and committed faith has led to a passionate and clear call to make the most of what he has been given responsibility for. Certainly not a workaholic that worships his work, but a strategic steward that develops and grows what he has. It is a focus on being a *faithful steward,* desiring to be real responsible for real things in the real world for the sake of a real God. Part of being faithful in his business is keeping an eye on the opportunities that occasionally arise that can impact the business. Ben is wise enough to know that not all good opportunities are necessarily good for his business. Opportunities must be able to enhance the mission to be considered "good" for his business; otherwise, they may serve as nothing more than distractions. And sometimes, distractions can be quite expensive.

One day, an opportunity came unexpectedly. Ben wasn't looking for it. But he was certainly prepared for it when it came. He saw that it connected some significant dots together with his vision and how to get there.

Ben had formed some very strong and strategic relationships through the years with other business owners. One was a commercial builder named Steve who was ten years younger than Ben. He was drawn to Ben and the vision he had for his growing real estate organization because Steve had also been growing through these same seasons and issues as well. Steve approached Ben about creating a partnership focusing on commercial development. Ben immediately saw how this joint venture fit in beautifully with his own vision of impacting the city. The two men of faith and business locked arms and became an incredible force of good for the community. Land was bought and developed. New office parks were built. Downtown urban remodeling took place. A mall went up in the suburbs. Countless jobs were created. Families were impacted. The city and community were blessed and benefited.

It was character and integrity on display. Skills and service in action. A visible expression of a faith-filled calling and vision. Stewardship so passionate and committed that you could really see it on display. So many good things were happening.

Ben was now sixty-two years old. He had been through quite a bit in his forty years of business. He had learned so much and grew so deep. Connecting his faith with his business interests had certainly provided solid leadership and influence that continued to expand and have an impact.

Ben sat back in his office chair and a smile came across his face as he thought about this journey that he had been on for the past few decades. The smile was not there because of what had been accomplished over the years. It was there because he knew what was to come.

The most impactful and influential years were right around the corner. He was transitioning to the next season of business and leadership.

And he couldn't wait to start.

The Season of Powerful Privilege

Ben has had his sights on the community for some years now. His business interests have grown in a steady, healthy, and continuous fashion. He has given and invested his time, wisdom, and resources into his key leaders in his organization, to his business partner Steve, and to the city that he calls home. But, as significant of an impact that his business has had on the city and numerous people who live there, he is still only one business owner out of thousands in the city.

So if Ben could multiply the leadership impact on his own organization by strategically investing into the key leaders within it, then couldn't the same type of impact happen throughout the city if he strategically invested in the lives of other business leaders?

This is the Season of Powerful Privilege. It is a time when Ben is utilizing his wisdom, accumulated and grown over the years, along with his reputation in the city and the strategic relationships in business and civil government, to create something incredibly powerful. Just as he trained, mentored, and coached so many in his own business, he was now going to train, mentor, and coach other business owners and entrepreneurs on how to connect their faith with their business interests. He wants to help others to develop a deeper faith, a better business, and a much greater impact.

Ben realizes this could not only be *powerful* in its impact but that it is an incredible *privilege* to lead it. Very few make it to this season. Many fail along the way, either by moral compromise or foolishness. Too many just simply give up and pursue comfort instead of greatness. Ben realizes it is an honor for him to help shape the trajectory of others' lives. It is taking on a role of a **Community Shepherd.** His calling is now focused on *finishing strong.* The objective: to impact the city through the marketplace.

Ben formed two groups. One was for younger business owners in their Season of Production. Another was for more seasoned business owners in their Season of Provision. Ben had developed materials and tools for each group.

The Production group would meet on the first Wednesday of each month from 8:00 a.m. until noon. Each month consisted of an hour focusing on "Theology in Work," an hour on "Building a Better Business," an hour on "Leadership," and a final hour on "Personal Challenges or Q&A." Once a month was also a Zoom conference call that was for group coaching. There was a monthly fee to be part of the group. It wasn't that Ben needed the money, but he also knew that when an investment is made, the attention and commitment go up. Ben loved leading these younger owners and helping them to connect their faith with their business. To think deeply about what God was calling them to do. To help them develop a solid mission. To help get them from where they were to where they believed God wanted them to go. He could also see when someone was struggling during this difficult season of life. Ben was able to navigate that season well, and he was a tremendous resource and mentor to those moving through those difficult days. Pointing a young couple to needed marriage counseling or distributing resources for parental help was not uncommon.

The Provision group met every third Wednesday of the month. This group also had strategic material to help them during this season of their business and leadership. However, this group met from 8:00 a.m. to 3:00 p.m. They still went through materials about theology, business, and leadership, but they also used the extra time to serve as a peer advisory group for each other. Specific issues, problems, or opportunities that individual group members had could be brought up for insights, advice, or recommendations. Because of the intimate nature of some of the issues, the group was limited to twelve members. Ben would also meet one-on-one with each member during the month for personal leadership and business coaching. This group also paid monthly for the membership, only it was quite a bit more than the younger group.

One of the great issues for business owners and executives is loneliness. Their colleagues or direct reports cannot relate to the owner's personal struggles, and his family and friends can't comprehend his business issues. He feels quite alone at the top. For those of faith, the isolation can be even more profound. These business veterans finally are in a place "where these people get me and what I am going through." The impact on these people was powerful. The results were staggering. The same things that happened in Ben's life were now being seen in the lives of so many more.

Because there was a major university in the city where Ben lived, his business reputation was well known there, especially in the College of Business. Ben was asked to teach a class on entrepreneurialism that met once a week for an hour. Knowing that to speak about faith and business integrating together would probably not be allowed, he taught on "Principle-Based Business Development." It was a hit with the students, especially with those who were Christians. They realized these principles did not originate on their own or even with Ben. Principles that are universal, transcendent, and timeless come from a Person who is just like those traits. *God.*

Ben offered to meet with anyone twice a month at a campus coffee shop from 7:00–8:00 p.m. Anyone could come and ask specific questions about faith in the marketplace. Ben would also ask what type of business the students thought God might be calling them into. When possible, he would connect the student with one of the business owners in his group who shared the same business interest. This would allow the student to shadow a business of their interest that was run by someone driven by faith. It was a great opportunity for mentoring and impacting many young people who desired to enter the marketplace and make a significant impact.

This season is somewhat busy for Ben. He controls his schedule well, and he doesn't feel overworked. He does feel greatly fulfilled and satisfied. The impact of other business leaders in the city was growing because someone took the time to give them attention, wisdom, and the truth. Ben considered himself to be privileged to be a part of such an endeavor for the past seven years. What a ride for him!

As he sat back in his office chair again one day, he looked back on the past seven years. A smile slowly spread across his face. There was a sense of deep satisfaction and fulfillment.

But he wasn't done yet. There was something else that was growing in his heart that absolutely had to get done. He wanted to finish strong.

And the smile got a little bigger.

Ben secured a large conference room for a luncheon. He invited the people attached to the significant and strategic relationships he had built and developed over the years. Business owners: men and women who were part of his coaching groups, pastors from churches, attorneys, doctors, and construction workers. They were all there because they knew Ben. The respect and admiration were palpable in the room.

When the lunch was finished, Ben approached the podium to speak. He talked about the integration of one's business interests with their faith. He quickly spoke of the various seasons of business and leadership development that are common to those who choose this path of faith-driven business. As he got close to the end, he talked about the city becoming a focus for impact and doing good.

A large monitor behind the podium showed two pictures of some property. One was a building in the heart of the university. The other was a ten-acre plot of commercial land in the newer expanding area of the city. Ben announced that he had purchased both. All the monies he collected from his coaching groups over the years went toward the down payment, and Ben provided the rest from his personal accounts. The building in the heart of the university was going to become a crisis pregnancy center. The ten acres of land was going to be the home for The Oasis—a place of rescue, protection, restoring, and releasing for women and children who are victims of sexual trafficking. The vision included a three-story building that would provide lodging, counseling, social services, and training to help victims transitioning back into life, recovered and restored. Also, part of The Oasis is twenty mobile home units to serve as living quarters for up to one year as the women recover from the hell they have been through.

This is when Ben made the big ask. This monumental mission was going to take a tremendous amount of people and resources. Ben was asking for their contributions and help. The crowd stood and created thunderous applause. The outpouring was amazing. So much so that Ben sat down and started to weep.

At one of the tables, a younger business owner said, "What in the world did I just witness?" To which an older entrepreneur, who was a close friend of Ben, replied, "That my friend, is the way things ought to be!"

A board was formed to oversee both projects. The board was comprised of people holding professional expertise and wisdom, who shared a passion for living out their faith in the marketplace. All of them had spent time with Ben at one time or another.

Ben. At one time, just a young man who wanted to start a business yet took his faith and trust in an incredible God seriously. Ben allowed God to give him a vision and called him to a mission in the marketplace. Ben allowed God to shape him, change him, and grow him. Ben became a man of impact because he served the God who saved the man, transformed the man, and then went with the man into the marketplace to make an impact everywhere he went.

Ben knew he was small. He also knew God was big. Really big. And Ben wanted to live his life in that reality.

Ben saw himself as a catalyst. He saw God use him to start things that others would then catch on and carry on. Ben mentored and coached some. Now, others were mentoring and coaching even more. Ben started some significant coaching groups, and those are now led by others. Eight of these groups can now be found throughout the city. The marketplace is being tremendously impacted by those who are following a sacred call to be part of a sacred mission.

The city is not quite the same.

In his office, Ben opens a drawer and pulls out an old, well-worn paperback. It was a book that was required reading for one of his freshman literature classes when he was in college. He opened it up to a bookmarked page and looked again at the highlighted quote, which he has read countless times:

"Life should not be a journey to the grave with the intention of arriving safely in a pretty and well-preserved body, but rather to skid in broadside in a cloud of smoke, thoroughly used up, totally worn out, and loudly proclaiming, 'Wow! What a Ride!'"

Ben knew that the quote was from Hunter S. Thompson, a famous journalist, author, and self-described hedonist. Looking at the quote from the faith perspective of calling and stewardship, Ben thought it could have easily been penned by the apostle Paul.

This was the kind of life Ben wanted to live. He wanted God to take him on the ride of his life. To end this vapor of a life with "Wow! What a Ride!"

Ben sat back in his chair and reflected on the ride he has been on.

And then slowly, that familiar smile began to form on his face.

It appears that the ride isn't over quite yet.

Chapter Twelve
THE CONCLUSION

(Or the start of a new beginning!)

There is an interesting dynamic in the storylines of literature and the cultures in which they are written. In the West, the storylines of most books, movies, and shows have a pattern of "Beginning . . . Middle . . . End." It is very linear in its presentation, taking the reader to a place very different from where the story began.

In Jewish or Hebrew literature, the storylines have a different pattern, which is primarily, "Beginning . . . Middle . . . Beginning." Here the flow of the story is circular, bringing the reader back to the beginning with a new outlook or perspective.

One example is the Bible. In the opening scenes, we read about God dwelling with man in a place called Eden. As we read through it, we learn about sin, separation, and death, God taking on flesh to become the sacrifice and Savior, people responding to Him or rejecting Him, and His final triumph over all of those who oppose Him. And then, it is back to the beginning of the story as He creates a new heaven and earth. God dwelling with man in a sinless home for all of eternity.

Beginning . . . Middle . . . to a New Beginning.

What a great story. What a great reality to be part of.

You have now come to the end of this book. You can view this time through two different lenses. One is to put the book on a shelf and decide this is the end of this story. Or, after reading through the story, you can decide that it's time for a new beginning.

You are back to the beginning with your story—only now, you can be on the path to an even better story of you.

There are some vital components that will help you on your way to a better story of yourself—things that will get you to where you want to go as you connect your faith with your business interests.

Content. The content of this book will help to lay a foundation on which you can build on. I believe that great leaders are great learners. As I have said earlier, there are numerous resources available on theology, business, and leadership. I have tried to give you a matrix to determine which resources are good and which are garbage. Which ones apply to where you are right now and which ones you must dig into down the road. As Paul wrote to the church in Corinth, "All things are lawful, but not all things are profitable. All things are lawful, but not all things build up" (1 Corinthians 10:23). To live well and finish well requires content that is profitable and that builds up. It's true for life. It's true for your business as well.

Community. One of the biggest problems for business owners of faith is loneliness. Many feel all alone in their quest to integrate faith and business. Feeling all alone on this quest is very normal. Going at it all alone is stupid. Being able to connect and talk to others going through this quest is encouraging, insightful, and so beneficial. Like-minded peers giving advice and help can increase the satisfaction and results you are looking for. That's why we created a private Facebook group called "The Kalos Business Group." Here you can find information, resource suggestions, and connect with key individuals to help you run this race well.

Coaching. Coaching has become one of the most impactful tools to take your business interests higher and faster. I have personally benefited from coaching so much that I currently have four different coaches helping me in various areas of my business interests so I can accomplish those things that God has placed in my heart to the very best of my ability. It is an incredible investment to your growth as a faith-led business owner that has a calling, a vision, a mission, and a passion to see it become a reality. You can find some much-needed help by going to our website at www.thekalosbuisnessgroup.

com. We want to help you accomplish the impact in your business, which God has placed in your heart.

This is the end of the book, but not the end of your story.
It's time for a new beginning.
It's time to let good things run wild!

The more I considered Christianity, the more I found that while it had established a rule and order, the chief aim of that order was to give room for good things to run wild.
G.K. Chesterton

ABOUT THE AUTHOR

Dr. Greg is a dental entrepreneur who has founded two large multi-doctor, multi-specialty dental clinics and has served on a pastoral team for over twenty years. As a speaker, writer, and coach, Dr. Greg integrates sound Biblical theology with business and leadership wisdom to allow others to have a significant impact on themselves, their businesses, homes, churches, and communities. Dr. Greg and his wife Laura live in Coralville, Iowa, where they have raised, nurtured, and loved their nine children.

A free ebook edition
is available with the
purchase of this book.

To claim your free ebook edition:

Visit MorganJamesBOGO.com
Sign your name CLEARLY in the space
Complete the form and submit a photo of
the entire copyright page
You or your friend can download the ebook
to your preferred device

A **FREE** ebook edition is available for you
or a friend with the purchase of this print book.

CLEARLY SIGN YOUR NAME ABOVE

Instructions to claim your free ebook edition:
1. Visit MorganJamesBOGO.com
2. Sign your name CLEARLY in the space above
3. Complete the form and submit a photo
   of this entire page
4. You or your friend can download the ebook
   to your preferred device

Print & Digital Together Forever.

Snap a photo

Free ebook

Read anywhere

Printed in the USA
CPSIA information can be obtained
at www.ICGtesting.com
JSHW022341140824
68134JS00019B/1621

9 781631 957598